First published in 2008
© Demos. Some rights reserved
Magdalen House, 136 Tooley Street,
London, SE1 2TU, UK

ISBN 978-1-906693-07-7
Copy edited by Susannah Wight, London
Series design by modernactivity
Typeset by Chat Noir Design, Charente
Printed by Lecturis, Eindhoven

Set in Gotham Rounded
and Baskerville 10
Cover paper: Arctic Volume
Text paper: Munken Premium White

it's a material world

world

Samuel Jones
John Holden

DEMOS

This pamphlet is dedicated to the memory of
Sir Derek Higgs (1944–2008), Trustee of the
Textile Conservation Centre Foundation from
1976 to 2008 and one of the Textile Conservation
Centre's most stalwart supporters.

Contents

Acknowledgements

Our first and greatest thanks go to the many individuals kind enough to spare their time during this research. A list of the organisations involved is provided in the appendices to this pamphlet.

We have benefited throughout from the advice and comments of the staff of the Textile Conservation Centre in Winchester, in particular Mary Brooks, Dinah Eastop, Nell Hoare and Frances Lennard. At Icon (the Institute of Conservation), Simon Cane, Diane Gwilt, Alison Richmond and Caroline Saye have provided invaluable comments and help – a special thanks to Alastair MacCapra, the former chief executive of Icon, for his advice, comments and assistance in the early stages of this research. Other individuals who have shared thoughts and conversations include Spike Bucklow, Karen Finch, Kate Foley, David Leigh and Dean Sully, whose experience and statistical research have been reference points throughout.

At Demos, Peter Bradwell and Peter Harrington have both taken time to comment on the draft. The research was ably assisted by Nicola Hughes, Amarjit Lahel and Athina Mermiri. The video made by Tom Silverstone about this pamphlet can be downloaded at www.youtube.com/demostv. Thanks to Aleksi Neuvonen at Demos Helsinki for drawing our attention to *talkoot*.

As ever, all errors and omissions remain our own.

Samuel Jones
John Holden
November 2008

Foreword

It's a Material World: Caring for the public realm is a call to arms. It is also a blueprint for the future, developed through collaboration with heritage and museum leaders, conservators, professional associations and educators concerned about the future of conservation.

Conservation today is at a crossroads. It has made great strides over the last half century evolving into a sophisticated, objective and scientifically based profession, trained for its vital role of caring for the nation's material heritage. For much of this evolution, the focus has been on developing and raising conservation standards and practices. It has necessarily been artefact-based – defined within a traditional museum framework. As a result the conservation profession has been relatively invisible, hidden away from government policy makers and more importantly the general public.

It worked for the times but the times have changed. The technological, social and economic changes of the twenty-first century are affecting the cultural sector. Although the value and importance of our material heritage is unaltered, the way that we interpret it and use resources is changing. As the guardians of this heritage, the conservation profession needs to be a partner in the decision-making process. Yet the profession's low public profile hinders its ability to have an impact where it matters.

This has become only too apparent in the recent closures of conservation courses at British universities and colleges. Skilled scientific and craft processes crucial to saving materials must be learnt and an ethical framework is essential to do it correctly. Where once we were the leading nation, conservation training in the UK is now under threat. In the face of this, what does the conservation workforce need to look like in 2020 and how can conservation education be strengthened? This crisis in conservation education has also become the rallying point for change in the profession and a desire to redefine it to make it relevant far into the future. The profession stands at a major crossroads; this paper gives direction, focus and a plan for how all involved can contribute.

One thing is clear: the conservation profession has to widen its scope, to look at the broader role conservation plays and embrace public engagement. Conservators have begun to build a role of wider value in society, evidenced by the many examples of public engagement in this report. This is certainly true at Historic Royal Palaces, where public communication has been integrated into every conservator's job and programmes such as 'Ask the Conservator' have been developed to engage visitor interest in our charitable cause.

We at Historic Royal Palaces depend on a highly skilled team of collection and building conservators. We welcome this report; we support a national strategy for change and we support broadening the professional role of the conservator. All conservation organisations, conservators, professional associations, research centres, education providers and government policy makers need to work together to open new ways to foster conservation. This will ensure its valuable role in society is strengthened, so that our material heritage remains meaningful for society today and in the future.

Michael Day
CEO, Historic Royal Palaces

Prologue: Standing on the shoulders of a giant

The Cerne Abbas Giant in Dorset is one of the most recognised heritage sites in the world. In the Second World War his chalk-white outline was dulled to prevent him being used as a landmark by German bombers and, in September 2008, when volunteers helped the National Trust conserve the Giant, it created headlines from Manhattan to Macau.[1]

Usually the Giant is conserved by allowing sheep to graze around his outline, but the recession had forced the local farmer out of business and no sheep were available. The National Trust turned to volunteers; members of the public came together from all over the country to care for a national symbol, trimming the grass and using chalk to preserve his outline. 'It's hard work,' said Chris Irish, a computer programmer who had made the 500-mile round trip from Leeds to spend two days caring for the Giant, 'but it's not often you get to work on an icon.'[2]

This pamphlet is about the value that Chris and others gain from caring for something that matters to them, and the value that all of us receive from acts of conservation.

Executive summary

It is only when people care about things that they get conserved. So in choosing what things to conserve, and how to conserve them, we simultaneously reflect and create social value. How things are kept and cared for demonstrates their significance not just as objects, buildings or landscapes, but in terms of how much value we place on them. What we conserve is a statement of what we respect, who we are and who we wish to be. Conservation therefore not only sustains and refreshes the values of the past – giving us an understanding of where we have come from – but also reflects values for the present and the future.

In addition to providing recommendations for conservators this pamphlet calls for action from policy makers, cultural professionals and the public. All of these groups have an interest in conservation and caring for the material world, and they all have a part to play in connecting conservation to some of the major challenges we face as a society, both in the UK and internationally.

On a professional level, the UK's conservators lead the world: objects are brought to the UK for conservation; over half of Europe's and many of the world's conservators are educated on the UK's conservation courses; and our conservation professionals work with colleagues from around the globe.

On a public level, engagement in conservation provides new ways to connect people with the public realm, but it also provides a space in which people can negotiate between the many values that we encounter in modern society. Public engagement in conservation is underpinned and made possible by conservation professionals who provide a professional framework, expertise and standards when caring for the material world. Much as the role of medical professionals is both to provide remedial healthcare and to help each of us live a healthier life, so conservators provide a paradigm not just for fixing things when they are broken, but for a wider social ethos of care, where we individually and collectively take responsibility and action.

However, at the moment in the UK this paradigm is threatened by a lack of policy attention and the low public profile of conservation. The interest that the public shows for conservation work that they see taking place in cultural institutions is not matched by public understanding and recognition of the profession in general.

This has a negative impact on the support that conservation gets from the wider cultural sector, and the support that politicians will show for it. For example, two of the leading conservation courses – which in some areas of expertise provide the only training available in the UK – have recently been threatened with closure. A third looks set to lose significant funding in 2011, and as budgets in higher education and the cultural sector are tightened, more closures could follow.

Part of the solution to conservation's low profile is that conservators themselves must find new ways to demonstrate the connection between their work and the wider social and cultural values that caring for the material world engenders. These values range from the very specific (such as the way that innovation in conservation practice spills over into technological advances in industrial processes) to the very general – picking up litter, for instance, is an act that conserves the quality of the public realm.

Recommendations

This pamphlet makes recommendations that will require action from policy makers, cultural professionals, conservators and the public alike.

The central recommendations of this pamphlet are that:

· conservators' work should be recognised as **integral not only to the culture and heritage sector but also to social well-being**

- **policy makers, cultural professionals and conservators
  should collaborate in communicating the importance of
  caring for the material world and its social benefits to a
  wider public**
- **conservators should build on existing practice in public
  engagement and connect their practice to wider agenda**
- **policy makers must support a conservation education sector
  that has flourished and has an international reputation that is
  second to none, but is currently under threat**
- conservators should **extend their existing involvement in
  social innovation.** Alongside communicating the importance
  of care, they can provide a logic that reinforces a less throw-away
  society, and the need to look after, rather than replace, goods –
  something which will be essential as we tackle the ills of
  pollution, climate change and environmental degradation.

These are some of the specific recommendations:

- The Department for Culture, Media and Sport (DCMS) should
  take the lead on **a new policy agenda focused on the social
  importance of caring for the material world;** this will address
  issues relating to the social importance of conservation, and
  sustaining the conservation sector.
- The initiative would be **coordinated by an Adviser who would
  convene a conservation steering group – the Material World
  Board** – comprising cultural professionals, educators, policy
  representatives and conservators.
- One of the steering group's core objectives should be to **sustain
  the UK's conservation education base for the future,** and
  **identify areas beyond the cultural industries in which
  conservation can be supported and encouraged to contribute
  to policy agenda at a cross-departmental level,** in particular
  communities and innovation. As well as a representative from
  DCMS, the steering group should include representatives from
  the Department for Business, Enterprise & Regulatory Reform
  (BERR), Communities and Local Government (CLG), the
  Department for Innovation, Universities & Skills (DIUS), the
  Department for Environment, Food and Rural Affairs (DEFRA)

and the new Department for Energy and Climate Change (DECC), and should also represent all the UK nations.

- Funding for larger-scale conservation projects should include the requirement of **a training component, providing and supporting on-the-job learning** at a range of levels, from novice to graduate professional.

- **Cultural leaders should champion the conservation sector** in public and in funding negotiations with DCMS, and this should be complemented by a **greater representation of conservation in exhibitions, and further initiatives from conservators in public engagement.**

- Developing some of the existing examples highlighted in this research, conservators should seek to use **public engagement and communication** to reflect the social importance of caring for the material world and reflect the different values, past and present, that objects represent.

- At least annually, **space should be devoted in every publicly funded museum for an object, contributed *and cared for* by a member of the public from the surrounding area that represents something of his or her community.**

- Conservators should **visit schools** as part of the government's pledge to provide 'five hours of culture' each week.

- Following the example of citizens' juries, in cases in which large amounts of public money will be spent on conservation, **conservation juries should be established to take into account public opinion on decisions made.** These would not be tasked with ultimate decision-making authority, but would be used to prioritise cases for conservation according to public interest, and would recommend how the public might be drawn into the process. The juries would reflect the public's rights, responsibilities and interests in relation to conservation. They would be chaired and managed by trained conservators, who report to the **Material World Board at DCMS**, and can provide the public jurors with professional judgement and advice.

- Conservators and cultural institutions should also encourage and supervise people in **volunteering to undertake non-interventive and preventive conservation work.**

- Finally, there should be a **nationwide initiative to communicate and celebrate the values of conservation.**

1 Caring for the material world

In 2006 the House of Lords Science and Technology Committee stated that 'under the current governance and funding structure, the maintenance of the science base for conservation, and with this the long-term preservation of the United Kingdom's cultural heritage, are severely under threat'.[3] Already, the University of Durham's MA Course in Archaeological Conservation had been forced to close temporarily. Since then, the situation has become more critical with the threat of closure of several of the leading centres of conservation education in the UK such as the Textile Conservation Centre at the University of Southampton and the decision of the Victoria & Albert Museum (V&A) to reduce funding for the course it runs jointly with the Royal College of Art (RCA) from 2011.

Conservation may seem to many a hidden and specialised activity, but in fact it underpins the material world. A society expresses and cements its values through its approaches to using, caring for and preserving objects that have significance, whether as fine art or for everyday use.

Bad government?

In about 1339 the artist Ambrogio Lorenzetti painted a series of frescoes in the Palazzo Pubblico in Siena, which are among the most important illustrations of political theory ever produced. As Geoff Mulgan, the former Director of the Cabinet Office's Strategy Unit, put it, they are 'the most brilliant depiction of the difference between good power and bad power'.[4]

In the paintings, when all is well with the government, trade flourishes, citizens dance in harmony and new buildings are constructed: even the countryside looks greener and its yield more plentiful. Under Bad Government, things implode: crops and citizens die, violence erupts and buildings crumble. What Lorenzetti is telling us is that the health of the polity and the state of the material world are intimately connected.

The frescoes amount to an early commentary on 'social capital', the term made famous by the US political scientist Robert Putnam, who defined it as 'social networks and the associated norms of reciprocity and trustworthiness'.[5] Social capital is the glue that holds us together as a society. In turn, social capital is anchored in the physicality of the material world around us, and in the objects and artefacts that we have produced throughout history. When we do not care for the world around us, it shows a poor sense of social responsibility and collective will, and is often a sign of worse to come – something recognised in policing, where low-level degradation of litter and graffiti is thought to encourage more serious crime.[6]

The consequences of damage to the material world are clear, from the deliberate destruction of the Bamiyan Buddhas or the English Reformation, to the accidental loss to fire of both major contemporary artworks at Momart in London and much-loved puppets at Aardman's studios in Bristol. But are we equally aware of the vast benefits of care? The UK lost a rich heritage in medieval art to iconoclasm, but have we been conscious enough of what remains, and what needs to be done to protect, preserve and communicate it?

At Djenné, in Mali, the mud walls of the famous mosque suffer regular erosion. Each year, the worshippers there take part in a ceremonial repairing of the buildings at this World Heritage Site (photo 1). At Djenné conservation is not a chore. It is a way of thinking and a way of being. It is a way of expressing values, reinforcing social bonds and confirming identity.

Caring for things helps us associate with the values that they represent. What lessons might we take from this in relation to *our* society in the UK? Here, we often think of conservation as relating primarily to the specialist treatment of objects, buildings and other items of cultural and heritage importance. It is true that we have world-class, dedicated and highly-trained professionals but do we value their work highly enough, and do we appreciate the role that they play in relation not only to the physical public realm, but also to our concepts of who we are? Moreover, is conservation something in which we can all participate? How would a widespread *attitude* of care and conservation improve our society? How can the values of respect, mutual effort and care lived out at Djenné and elsewhere be brought to play in our communities?

Conservation has a significant role to play in policy making. For over a decade, policy makers and political scientists have been preoccupied with a perceived decline of social capital. Almost echoing Lorenzetti, Richard Sennett, a prominent observer of the modern day polity, has written that 'participation in the *res publica* today is most often a matter of going along, and the forums for this public life, like the city, are in a state of decay'.[7]

Such concerns seem a world away from the conservation studio, but they are not.

Caring for English 'icons'

In 2006 the DCMS's pilot programme Culture Online offered people in England the chance to nominate things that they thought represented Englishness.[8] The result was a list of 75 icons, some of which are material, others abstract. Of this list, almost a third has undergone direct material conservation, including the Lindisfarne Gospels, the Magna Carta, HMS Victory *(whose only surviving sail was conserved by the now-threatened Textile Conservation Centre), the Sutton Hoo helmet and Constable's* The Hay Wain. *The list demonstrates how intrinsic conservation is to our sense of identity.*

Caring for 'Icons' like those on the DCMS's list is about more than simply the preservation of heritage. It is a statement about what is valued and why. With this realisation, the conclusions of the House of Lords Science and Technology

Committee, and the threatened closure of several of the leading conservation courses in the UK provide a wake-up call. It is not just the culture and heritage sectors that will lose out should the threat to conservation become real, but so will the public realm as a whole.

2 Conservation and its values

The idea of conservation

The *Oxford English Dictionary* defines conservation as 'to keep in safety, or from harm, decay, or loss; to preserve with care; now usually, to preserve in its existing state from destruction or change'.[9] But conservation is not just about practice, it is also an idea and an attitude, and is about choices. Decisions as to what to treat, how to treat it, and whom to involve are rooted in the relationship conservators perceive between the object and its social context. In a white paper, *Heritage Protection for the 21st Century*, DCMS and the Welsh Assembly recognised this:

Designation [the identification of those aspects of our past that are most important to us and explaining why they are important] is the first step in an effective heritage protection system. It is a means of identifying those aspects of our past that are most important to us, and explaining why they are important. Effective designation is also the basis for decisions about the way we manage change to the historic environment.[10]

Value is socially determined: an object, artefact or building can only have value insofar as people give it value. Conservation is therefore rooted in social action, and refers to the *management* of change in objects that have fluctuating value in the society in which they exist. It is in conservation's favour that it is *not* objective. Conservation is about refreshing and renewing culture and heritage in ways that reflect and contribute to society's values, thereby making a statement about value to others, and a statement about the present to the future. Objects matter because they are powerful visual metaphors that can bypass language. At heart, conservation is a political act – it is a contribution to a conversation between values[11] (see box 1).

Conservation is rooted in professional practice, but extends well beyond it. As a report produced by the Getty Conservation Institute in California, a leading centre for conservation research and practice, put it:

Traditional conservation remains the core of the field's activity and its raison d'être, but... the conservation process is best seen more inclusively, encompassing the creation of heritage, interpretation and education, the many efforts of individuals and social groups to be stewards of heritage, and shifting economics and political tides, as well as more traditional practices of conservators, preservationists, curators and other professionals.[12]

Box 1

A professional's definition of conservation

A good definition of conservation, which takes conservation beyond the OED definition, is provided by Dean Sully, a lecturer in conservation at University College, London, who sees conservation involving interpretation as much as preservation. He says that conservation is:

a complex and continual process that involves determining what heritage is, how it is cared for, how it is used, by whom, and for whom. Conservation as a developing social practise is not only concerned with definitions of best practise, but in continually reassessing the applicability of new approaches to changed circumstances... Conservation is a process of understanding and managing change rather than merely an arresting process; it is a means of recreating material cultural heritage that seeks to retain, reveal and enhance what people value about the material past and sustain those values for future generations... objects are conserved because they are valued for the effect they have on people.[13]

Conservation has a fundamental place within the cultural and heritage sector, and a special relationship with science. In presenting evidence to the House of Lords Science and

Technology Committee, the British Museum positioned the conservation sector 'at the interface of the arts and sciences; scientific examination, analysis and research inform an understanding of material culture and the susceptibility of artefacts to change, while historical, archaeological and art historical research place these results in the context of place, period, practice and belief – a two-way knowledge transfer across this often problematic interface'.[14] In fact, conservation is one way in which people can make the connection between the arts and the sciences.

3 The UK conservation sector

The conservation profession

In the UK conservation professionals are part of the culture and heritage sector. They work in a range of contexts and in relation to a range of materials that comprise our historic and cultural environment, and without their work much would be inaccessible to the public. They are specialists, and their practices range from the conservation of fine art painting to riveting in the case of historic ships, and from building conservation to caring for manuscripts in our libraries and many more. Without conservators many of our greatest treasures would be inaccessible or – worse still – non-existent.

Full steam ahead

Launched in 1843, the SS Great Britain *is one of the nation's finest surviving ships, the work of one of the great figures of our past – Isambard Kingdom Brunel, who came second in a poll to choose Great Britons conducted by the BBC in 2002 – and also a major technological leap in the history of human achievement. However, in 1995, analysis by conservators of the hull estimated that, within 25 years, it would become structurally unsafe and inaccessible to visitors.*

To preserve the hull, and make it safe for visitors, the SS Great Britain Trust decided to create an envelope around the ship to control the atmosphere. They also took the opportunity to reconsider the way that visitors could relate to the ship. The result was to 'float' the ship in its dry dock by placing a transparent 'roof' at what would have been water level. This not only created a new visitor experience, providing an image of what the ship would have looked like as a working vessel, but also met conservation needs in relation to the hull. At the same time, the project provided an opportunity for people to learn more about conservation, because the hardware that controls the atmosphere has been incorporated into the display and hence the biography of the SS Great Britain. The result is that first-year visitor numbers exceeded predictions by 54 per cent. 'It is the best museum I've ever been to precisely because it never feels like a museum at all. All museums should be like this,' said one member of the public. Conservation, and the constructive use of conservation in communication, put one of the UK's most valued and valuable heritage treasures not just on an even keel, but on the crest of a wave. See photos 2 and 3.

Within the cultural sector, the relationship between conservators and curators has been changing over the last two decades. Whereas in 1989, according to the then Director of the British Museum, museum curators were 'sometimes impatient of the narrow parameters laid down by conservators', now conservators are recognised as contributing to the understanding of objects, as well as being essential to the delivery of major government-funded building and refurbishment projects in our museums and galleries.[15] As the late Anne d'Harnoncourt, Director of the prestigious Philadelphia Museum of Art, observed: 'what gives the public trust [in cultural and heritage institutions] overall is a sense that things are being thoughtfully and responsibly handled by people who care a great deal about them'.[16]

The conservation profession in the UK

In the UK the conservation workforce comprises:

· practitioners working in the public sector and in institutions like museums and libraries and organisations like English Heritage, Historic Scotland and the National Trust[17]
· private practitioners, either working alone or in small to medium-sized companies

- professionals engaged in research and teaching conservation within the UK's higher education institutions (HEIs) and other educational organisations

These areas often interact to a high degree. For example, some conservation centres in HEIs undertake contract work and have developed project-based income sources, while conservators working in public sector institutions are also often engaged in academic research and education.

The public sector

It is estimated that roughly half of conservators are employed in major museums and other cultural and heritage organisations. They range from heads of department through to specialist and assistant conservators and, at the entry points of the sector, interns. In a small number of cases, and under professional supervision, members of the public work on simpler, more straightforward – and, as a rule, non-interventive and preventive – conservation tasks such as documentation and others relating to the upkeep of properties and artefacts, like storage and dusting.

Most of the major national and cultural institutions – including the British Library, the National Museum of Wales, the National Museums of Scotland, the National Gallery in London and the Natural History Museum – have conservation studios. Throughout the country, larger regional museums also employ conservators. In at least one case at Birmingham Museum and Art Gallery, bench-space and facilities are rented out to private sector practitioners.

Alongside such larger culture and heritage institutions, organisations like the National Trust and English Heritage are also significant employers of conservators. In addition, both use volunteers to fulfil tasks that do not require high-level conservation skills and knowledge; volunteers thus support and complement the professional activities of employed conservators. At the National Trust, volunteers are an integral part of the conservation workforce, while volunteering provides an entry point to the sector. As Katy Lithgow, Head Conservator at the National Trust, observed, it 'could not operate without volunteers... and they can be inspired by their experience with us to [undertake training to] become the conservators and conservation managers of the future'.[18]

The public sector is also important in making people aware of conservation. First, objects and buildings themselves are seen to be receiving treatment – the Tower of London is a recent high-profile example (see chapter 5). Second, there is an increasing trend for institutions to use conservation as a way of engaging the public. In 1996, for example, National Museums Liverpool opened the National Conservation Centre to the public, and this was followed by the opening in 2007 of the British Library Centre for Conservation, which was specifically 'designed to make a quintessentially core, but "back room", activity more "front of house"'.[19] Scheduled to open in 2011, the northwest extension planned for the British Museum will also feature public displays of conservation. This will continue a theme in the British Museum's public programme. In 2008, 'Conservation in Focus' was a special exhibit in which conservators worked on objects in a gallery by the entrance to the museum. Alongside programmed talks, members of the public could also ask conservators what they were doing and how – some asked how they could become involved in conservation (photo 4).[20]

The private sector

Private sector practitioners operate in the marketplace of conservation, undertaking commissions from organisations like museums or auction houses, and from private clients and institutions. One of the largest, Plowden & Smith in London, employs about 20 people and offers a range of conservation services. Individual practitioners tend to specialise in specific media, like stained glass, textiles or ceramics.

Private practitioners treat and advise on objects ranging from small-scale private commissions to larger-scale public work. For example, when three Qing Dynasty Chinese vases were accidentally smashed by a visitor to the Fitzwilliam Museum in

2006, conservation treatment was carried out by a private practitioner.[21] Due to museum overheads, the degree of specialist expertise required for a particular job and the range of object types, conservation professionals interviewed for this research estimated that about 70 per cent of interventive conservation in the public sector is now contracted out to private practitioners. According to interviewees for this research, there is a trend within museums to allocate resources to the conservation of objects for special display or short-term loans rather than to care for the overall collection, and to contract this exhibition-led work out to the private sector.

Establishing oneself as a private practitioner requires experience, reputation and references. Although not yet essential, all those working as professional conservators are encouraged to participate in Icon's Professional Accreditation of Conservator-Restorers (PACR) scheme (see box 2) and those wishing to be listed on Icon's *Conservation Register* must be accredited. For many starting out in the sector, work experience with a recognised and senior practitioner provides valuable practical training, which enhances qualifications gained through a university degree or other formal learning programme. However, the cost implications for a private practitioner in supporting a learner are significant.

Higher education institutions

A third important area of conservation is within higher education. There are currently 13 centres of conservation education in the UK, which act both as education centres for the conservation workforce of the future and as research centres for the development of the subject and discipline. Mostly, these are housed in HEIs, which award the degrees. For example, the Textile Conservation Centre is currently part of the University of Southampton, and the Hamilton Kerr Institute for painting conservation is part of the University of Cambridge.

At the moment, postgraduate education is the normal entry route to practising as a professional conservator, and Masters' degrees are often seen as a requirement for professional work. In

Europe, MA level education is the minimum required to work as a conservation professional.[22] If European education is to be more compatible and comparable under the Bologna Process, this will pose problems for the future, limiting the transferability of British-trained conservators' skills and their prospects of employment.[23] As mentioned above, Icon operates an accreditation scheme, which allows for practitioners from formal education programmes or apprenticeship routes to demonstrate competence against a set of professional standards (see box 2). The centres of education are important because they provide both the intellectual underpinning of the sector and are also the primary means of teaching the theory and practice of conservation in an integrated way. Alongside the work carried out in culture and heritage institutions, they also play a vital role in research and innovation.

The professionalisation of the conservation sector

While conservators often fulfil clear roles in organisations, and their individual expertise in dealing with different materials is well understood, historically there has been a lack of clarity about how the private sector, the public sector and HEIs come together as a conservation sector.[24] For conservation to gain support at the political level, and for conservation to attract the public attention it deserves, attaining such clarity will be essential.

Clarity and consistency are being achieved through the formation of Icon, which was established by amalgamating several smaller professional bodies in June 2005. Icon is the lead voice for the conservation of cultural heritage in the UK. Icon embraces the wider conservation community, incorporating not only professional conservators but all others who share a commitment to improving understanding of and access to our cultural heritage. It has 3,000 individuals and organisations in the private and public conservation sectors and HEIs. Icon acts as a figurehead and representative at policy level within the cultural and heritage sector. It provides logic to structures like accreditation and knowledge management, as well as playing an important role in knowledge transfer through its publications and events. Icon also runs *The Conservation Register*, a centralised resource for locating conservators and conservation services in the private sector by specialisation and location which, because those listed on it must be accredited, also functions as a validation of professionals within the sector.[25]

Box 2   **Icon's PACR scheme**

The Professional Accreditation of Conservator-Restorers (PACR) is the professional practice assessment for conservation professionals wishing to gain accredited status. The scheme is run by Icon, in association with the Society of Archivists and the British Horological Institute. It is the principal professional qualification in conservation-restoration, demonstrating that a practitioner is a fully-qualified and capable professional. It is available to would-be practitioners regardless of their educational background or ability to fund and attend higher education. The PACR framework applies a common standard across the profession, regardless of the route taken to reach a professional level of capability, the specialism or the context in which the conservator practises. Operating across a 'Novice to Expert Scale', the framework identifies competencies ranging from 'unlikely to be satisfactory unless closely supervised' through to 'excellence achieved with relative ease'.

Acting as a means for conservators to demonstrate proficiency and a guide to prospective employers and those commissioning conservation, PACR is becoming adopted throughout the sector, with institutions like the V&A specifying PACR levels in job applications.

PACR presents the professional face of conservation in terms that can easily be understood. It demonstrates the knowledge, skills and attitudes of the conservator, and provides an intelligible 'route-map' of progression for those seeking to enter the workforce.[26]

Between them, the private and public sectors and HEIs provide the infrastructure for the conservation sector. With the establishment of Icon and the implementation of PACR standardisation, there is now a sound professional base for conservation in the UK. This is the platform from which to build appreciation of the wider public benefits that conservation generates. However, as the next chapter shows, the bedrock on which that platform is built is fragile and pressures on conservation education in particular could cause it to crumble.

4 Conservation under threat

The closure of conservation education courses

It is a great irony that, just as the importance of conservation in relation to our public realm is becoming clear and the profession has taken shape, several leading education centres for the conservation sector have been forced to close. In 2005 the Durham course in archaeological conservation was shut; it has only recently been announced that it will reopen in 2009. This was followed in relatively quick succession by the announcement in 2007 that, unless an alternative source of funding or home could be found, the Textile Conservation Centre (TCC) at the University of Southampton would face a similar fate; at the time of writing, the TCC is in the process of negotiating a plan for its future – but the outcome of these negotiations is far from certain. Elsewhere, the V&A has reduced the amount of resources it will contribute from 2011 to the MA conservation course it has run jointly with the RCA since 1989.

The underlying reasons for these closures and pressures are economic. The University of Southampton's decision to close the Centre was because 'postgraduate conservation education is a resource-intensive activity'.[27] The equipment and materials of conservation are expensive and the studio-space required is large, especially for artefacts like textiles; furthermore, because students often work on objects of historic and artistic importance, there are also security costs to bear in mind. Staff-to-student ratios are of necessity low (because many skills have to be learned on a one-to-one basis), and thus costly to maintain. Couple this with the sector's emphasis on postgraduate qualifications and the attendant cost implications for prospective students, and it is easy to see how conservation education does not easily fit into an economy of higher education in which student numbers and the fees that they bring are required to balance the bottom line. The combined pressures of the economy of universities and the costs of conservation courses simply do not square: several of the people interviewed for this paper think it likely that other courses will soon find themselves in the same boat as the TCC.[28]

Why the crisis in conservation education matters

Education is the bedrock of any profession. Damage to the education that underpins the conservation sector is worrying because the closure of centres of excellence will:

· erode the skills base of the sector
· reduce innovation in the sector
· lead to a loss of leadership
· damage the UK's international reputation as a leader in conservation
· damage the idea of conservation in the UK

These factors are also inter-related and so the effects are likely to be magnified. Overall, their effect will be to reduce the wider social value that conservation adds. Without leaders in the sector, it will be difficult to gain greater support for conservation and conservation education, in turn further damaging the skills base and stemming the supply of conservation educators for the future. Without the innovation that research centres provide, it will be difficult for the sector to respond to the changes that we are witnessing in the world, from strains on natural resources to the damage to heritage caused by climate change. However, each also has significant implications in its own right.

The erosion of the skills base of the sector

Cuts in education will reduce the workforce of the future and that means that heritage and culture in the UK will suffer. The current workforce is ageing and, eventually, there will be fewer trained conservators to fill jobs. At the British Library, 'of the 58 book conservators, 16 will reach retirement age within the next 5 years, 40 within 10 years and 54 in 15 years... to maintain the status quo in the British Library alone, a minimum of 4 new conservators must be recruited every year'.[29] Furthermore, as research progresses and conservators have increasingly to work with different and new materials, like digital records or man-made fibres and synthetics, conservation departments will constantly need both to recruit staff and graduates with new skills, and find training opportunities for existing employees to update theirs. To answer this need, the British Library has developed an agreement with Camberwell College of Arts to act as an 'industry partner' in a foundation course on book conservation as well as having undertaken a skills audit to identify training needs in relation to the changing nature of the Library's collection, for example with regard to digital and sound collections. It has also established training for staff leading to the UK's NVQ (national vocational qualification) Level 3 in *training the trainers* to prepare staff; at the same time members of staff have volunteered to give public tours and have accordingly received customer service training.[30] However, this has required administration and resources unavailable to most institutions.

The loss of courses also has severe implications for the private sector: private sector practitioners need to be educated and trained just as much as those who work in the public and education sectors. A further threat exists in relation to large-scale work that is currently undertaken by the education centres and which the private sector could not replicate. For example, the conservation treatment carried out by the TCC on nineteenth-century painted linen scenery from the Normansfield Theatre in Teddington in Middlesex, some of which measure 35 square metres, required space and labour beyond the capacity of most in the private sector (photo 5). The work was significant because the theatre is part of Normansfield Hospital, founded in 1868 by Dr John Langdon Down, for the care of people suffering from what became known as Down's Syndrome. Theatre and music were vital to the hospital's educational programme and it is now widely recognised as one of the most important private theatres in Britain.[31]

The reduction of innovation in the sector

Research and education in conservation also matters because it can be a space for innovation more generally. If leading centres of specialisation close, then in the future there will be a shortage of skills in specific areas. Specialist centres function as centres of research, and their closure threatens to undermine the knowledge base of the future – the TCC, for instance, has pioneered research into the longevity of man-made textiles and challenged assumptions about their durability.

The counter-argument – that the academic research gap can be filled by conservators working in our public institutions – will not bear scrutiny. As the Director of the British Museum Neil MacGregor pointed out to the House of Lords Science and Technology Committee, 'for anybody having to manage a museum or a gallery budget, research is obviously one of the areas you can most easily cut back on because the impact is not immediately visible'.[32] Conversely, research can have beneficial resource implications. Finding out what environmental parameters are acceptable for maintaining collections can save energy costs. Research can help to focus resources on specific needs. Furthermore, without the education base in the first place, eventually, professionals working in institutions simply will not have the training to undertake the research.

Innovation through conservation

Techniques developed in conservation often have wider application. Conservators working on the Mary Rose *developed new ways of isolating DNA that went on to have significant impact in police forensic work.*

As the magazine British Archaeology *put it, 'without the* Mary Rose, *the science of DNA analysis from archaeological remains might not exist at all. In 1990 pig DNA was isolated from a pig bone from the ship: hardly startling in itself, but this was the first occasion on which the genuine survival of DNA from an archaeological specimen of known date had been proven, and was crucial in the development of forensic science.'*[33]

The loss of leadership

Organisations like the RCA, the Hamilton Kerr Institute and the TCC are not only leaders in research, but also international figureheads for conservation. Staff in conservation education centres publish papers and books that communicate and encourage innovation in the sector, provide the means by which fellow professionals can update techniques used, and also contribute to the UK's reputation in what is a global sector.[34]

Alongside conservation leaders within the public sector, the staff of conservation education centres also contribute to the public face of conservation, which will become ever more important as the sector's value becomes clearer. Thought leadership from conservation educators in relation to public engagement was a central feature of the 2008 International Institute of Conservation Conference on Conservation and Access.[35] As discussed in chapter 9, such activity will have a significant impact on the sector's ability to raise its public and political profile. Within the higher education system, conservation leaders also encourage potential students to enrol in courses which will be vital to the sector's survival and development.

The damage to the UK's international reputation

The UK's conservation training centres have international repute. When the threat of the TCC's closure was announced, the ripples were felt on the other side of the world. An article in *The Times* entitled 'Textile conservation centre stitched up' attracted comments from the many countries whose professionals have either trained at or benefited from the TCC's expertise. 'Does the British government actually know, which [sic] fatal consequences the closing of the TCC would have for Britain's Cultural Heritage?' asked one reader from Austria. From Dunedin, another wrote, 'the closure of the TCC will not only cause an enormous loss of expertise in the UK, but also have an impact on the rest of the world. New Zealand institutions and individuals often rely on the skills, knowledge and training of TCC conservators for the preservation of textile heritage. The TCC's teaching and ground-breaking research, as well as the students they produce, are considered a bench-mark for excellence in the conservation community. How can such achievement be rewarded with closure?'[36] Certainly, history holds a warning. In 2003 the University of Canberra closed its conservation training programme but, by 2008, the decision had been made to reopen it. In the course's absence, the university realised that it had lost benefits in prestige and cross-pollination with other courses. The problem was that, in the meantime, available staff had gone and huge costs were incurred in replacing the equipment and other resources that had been lost and sold on.[37]

The TCC is not unique in its international impact: many of the alumni of the RCA and V&A now work in places as varied as Bangkok and New York.[38] The loss of conservation courses will therefore have an impact that is far from localised within the conservation sector. It has serious implications for society at large and the UK's international reputation.

The damage to the idea of conservation in the UK

The loss of conservation skills would have a knock-on effect in relation to the values that conservation contributes to society. Skills are more than the bedrock of a sector: they are the starting point of a culture that extends beyond that sector. Society is structured around a multitude of different sectors, and those sectors embody values.[39] For example, doctors and the medical profession are the reference points for healthcare; the police represent order; and politicians embody the debate on which the institutions of democracy are built. Professions provide standards and frameworks within which we exist, and which we develop by challenging. The same is true for the conservation sector. It is from the values that conservators embody that we can understand the importance of sustaining the material world. If the conservation sector is to engage the public in the idea of conservation, then it must be seen to have political backing both from the leaders of the cultural and heritage sector and from Westminster.

Innovative support for conservation – the Great East Window at York Minster

A good example of how policy makers and funders support the heritage and conservation sector can be seen in how the Heritage Lottery Fund (HLF) assisted the conservation of the Great East Window at York Minster. The window is probably the first piece of art by a named master in England and is considered one of the most important examples of stained glass in the world. However, it is not in good condition, and much earlier but poor restoration made it difficult to appreciate its full splendour.

The condition of the window itself is matched by the condition of training opportunities for historic glass conservators. Having identified this gap, the HLF funded the York Glaziers Trust to train two new apprentice glass conservators, who will develop skills by working alongside professionals on the East Window itself, providing the workforce necessary to complete so big and important a task. They will then be able to transfer their skills to the treatment of other examples of stained glass.

Not only will this help tackle the shortage of trained glass conservators in the UK, but it also provides support for the conservation professionals in providing training. Taking on apprentices or trainees is an expensive job for any conservator: it demands time and effort, and this is particularly burdensome in the conservation sector. As well as awarding the Minster £10 million towards a major conservation scheme, the HLF was also able to provide leadership, by developing a model whereby training is incorporated into a major project.

The Long Tail of conservation

Conservation is not high in the public and political imagination. In exhibitions, we see the fruits of the conservator's work, but it is less often that we see their work itself.[40] More often than not, when the conservation of heritage and culture does come to public attention, it is in relation to work done to repair damage. Recent examples abound, from the restoration work being done on the *Cutty Sark*, which suffered extensive fire damage in 2007, to the restoration of the National Trust property Uppark, similarly gutted by fire in 1989.

In stories like these, the focus tends to be on the idea of large-scale repair, which casts conservation as something of a retrospective profession, called in when something has gone wrong. On top of that, conservation is often perceived as being limited to a technical and professional practice and, even then, that practice is poorly understood.

In fact, every day, throughout the country, countless small-scale preventive interventions and treatments are undertaken that are unseen and unrecognised. Often they relate to things of personal or sentimental importance, like samplers that are family heirlooms or work on buildings that preserve our material heritage. Individually, these often don't amount to much, but collectively they amount to a lot.

In 2004 the journalist Chris Anderson described a new way of understanding our behaviour, and the marketplace in particular; he called it the 'Long Tail'. He argued that internet consumerism has shifted the nature of markets for things like books and entertainment from being one determined by providers, to one utterly dominated by consumers. As the opportunities to purchase books, music, videos and other media have multiplied, markets are driven by niche interests that taken individually attract far fewer sales than mainstream and blockbuster titles; however, en masse, they drive a new market. 'For too long', Anderson wrote, 'we've been suffering the tyranny of lowest-common-denominator fare... many of our assumptions about popular taste are actually artefacts of poor supply-and-demand matching – a market response to inefficient distribution.'[41] For Anderson, 'the theory of the Long Tail can be boiled down to this: our culture and economy are increasingly shifting away from a focus on a relatively small number of hits (mainstream products and markets) at the head of the demand curve, and moving toward a huge number of niches in the tail... the true shape of demand is revealed only when consumers are offered infinite choice'.[42]

Applying the Long Tail theory to conservation reveals that

Figure 1 **The Long Tail applied to conservation**[43]

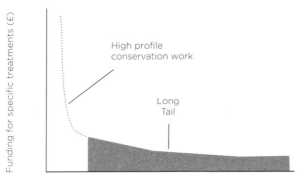

Number of heritage objects and artefacts in the UK

beyond the high-profile, large-scale works such as the cleaning of St Paul's Cathedral, or the work carried out on Holbein's *The Ambassadors* at the National Gallery, there are hundreds of thousands of smaller-scale conservation efforts. Figure 1 represents the Long Tail in a diagrammatical form.

The DCMS Icons list shows that the treatment of high profile objects and buildings will always be a necessity. In the capital alone, St Paul's and the Tower of London have both undergone conservation work over the past few years. However, the Icons list also includes items like 'the pint of real ale', a more everyday piece of our heritage whose sustenance is the direct concern of organisations like CAMRA, the Campaign for Real Ale. Conservation is about maintaining the values with which people identify, and refreshing them in ways that maintain their relevance.

Thinking in terms of a Long Tail of conservation shows that high profile examples are the tip of an iceberg that is in danger of melting. In the long run, not only will it be difficult to find professionals with enough training to care for the more celebrated examples of our culture, but the first hit will be the small-scale, more individual parts of our heritage – everyday treasures – such as objects in local museums and private possessions.

5   The current contribution of conservation

The Long Tail gives us an idea of the scale of the severe threat to the UK's cultural heritage that the House of Lords Committee identified. However, this is only half the story. If the warnings are not heeded, it won't just be the conservation sector that loses out. Conservation brings tremendous benefit to the UK in a number of policy areas and these will be undermined as well.

Culture is of value in its own right and the value of culture can be articulated on its own terms. But culture can also be described in terms of the effects that it produces in society and the economy.[44] In relation to conservation, four of the major effects are on:

· living together
· building cultural literacy
· cultural diplomacy
· encouraging tourism

Living together

Intercultural dialogue and the negotiation of cultural differences are integral to good community relations in the UK. This has translated into policy making and in 2007 CLG announced the findings of the Commission on Cohesion and Integration, *Our Shared Futures*. The Commission recommended specifically that 'cultural development agencies, including the Arts Council and the Heritage Lottery Fund, should require applicants for funding to demonstrate their commitment to integration and cohesion outcomes as part of their funding criteria'.[45]

The conservation sector contributes to the achievement of CLG's aims. Initiatives like the Hirayama Asian pictorial art conservation studio at the British Museum demonstrate the reflection of cultures at the international level and to diaspora communities within the UK. It is the only one of its kind in Europe, and is run by a conservator who trained and worked in Shanghai Museum for over 15 years.[46] Another example is the National Trust's work at Clandon Park in Surrey, where the diaspora Maori community is involved in conservation work.

Conservation and living heritage

Hinemihi, a Maori meeting house, sits in the garden at Clandon Park, and is the only complete ancestral Maori meeting house in Britain, and one of only four outside New Zealand. A meeting house is an embodiment of tribal ancestors, and so caring for a meeting house is highly symbolic. The Hinemihi project group, which undertakes conservation on the meeting house, is a collaboration between the London Maori community, Ngāti Hinemihi (Hinemihi's spiritual descendants in New Zealand), the National Trust (as stewards of Hinemihi), and others interested in Hinemihi's well-being. The project reveals the power of conservation to blend the living present with the past. On the one hand, the conservation process restores Hinemihi as the focal point of a community, and provides the London Maori with a space to connect to their own heritage; on the other, it enables the general public to engage with Maori world views and beliefs.

From the Maori perspective, caring for Hinemihi requires using the best available materials in her upkeep, and these might not be ones that are authentic to the period at which Hinemihi was originally constructed and brought to the UK (the nineteenth century). The project therefore represents a negotiation between the values of material and intangible heritage. Which is being conserved: the idea of Hinemihi and her value in the heritage and sustenance of Maori beliefs and rights, or her aesthetic and historic value as an artefact of the nineteenth century?[47] Hinemihi also reveals the potential of conservation to engage audiences and communicate living values effectively. See photos 6 and 7.

Building cultural literacy

According to the Nobel laureate Amartya Sen,

[by] supporting historical excavations and related research, development programmes can help to facilitate a fuller appreciation of the breadth of – and internal variations within – particular cultures and traditions. History often includes much greater variety of cultural influences and traditions than tends to be allowed by intensely political – and frequently ahistorical – interpretations of the present. When this is the case, historical objects, sites and records can help to offset some of the frictions of confrontational modern politics.[48]

As we encounter different cultures with greater frequency in all contexts, Sen's comments have wider application.

Cultural literacy is the ability to read and adapt to the many different cultures that we encounter in an interconnected world.[49] We need to broaden curricula not only to include knowledge about those cultures, but also to encourage an understanding of cultural forms (from the objects we look at in museums, to the media we see and the food we eat in the streets) as conveying something about people's identity and attitudes. This will require greater collaboration between policy makers, cultural institutions, cultural academics and education at all levels, and conservation has a role to play.

Government policy on culture and education is helpful in this regard. In February 2008 DCMS and the Department for Children, Schools and Families (DCSF) announced funding totalling £135 million to provide 'young people in England [with] the chance to experience high quality arts and culture'.[50] Announced as part of the 'Find your talent scheme', operated by a new body, the Youth Culture Trust, the aim is to provide all children, by 2010, with 'five hours of arts and culture a week, in and outside of the school day', a proposal linked to the Creative Britain initiative discussed in chapter 9.

The conservation sector can play a valuable role. By working with schools, conservators can help children learn and develop the skills and awareness necessary to care for and value the material world around them and in so doing contribute to the teaching of other subjects in the curriculum, from art and history to sciences like biology and chemistry. In the long term, this will contribute to the development of public awareness that is needed if the sector is to flourish and fulfil its potential. Furthermore, working with schools presents an ideal opportunity for young conservation professionals to develop skills of public engagement.

Cultural diplomacy

The shock with which the announcement of the decision to close the TCC was met around the world sits uncomfortably alongside the current policy focus on cultural diplomacy. In his first speech as Foreign Secretary, David Miliband spoke of 'using our strengths so that we are a force for good for Britain by being a force for good in the world' and of a foreign policy that is 'about values and interests together'. Specifically, he identified 'culture that is globally admired' as being one of the UK's greatest strengths.[51] Conservation relates directly to both these comments.

In January 2008 DCMS announced the launch of the World Collections Programme: £3.2 million allocated to a consortium of national museums for transnational cultural collaboration, building links and making the connections that will bolster Britain's international position.[52] Launching the fund, James Purnell, then Secretary of State for Culture, said:

[We] live in a shrinking world with more contact between cultures and countries than ever before. We need to learn how to live side by side, giving dignity to our differences and understanding our similarities. London's museums are one of the best places in the world to understand those different cultures. But we can deepen that understanding by creating connections with other museums around the world.[53]

The Programme will take two forms:

- communicating with others through culture
- consolidating the UK's position as a leading centre of cultural professionalism

Conservation is one of the most internationalised parts of the cultural sector and contributes to both:

· *Communicating through culture and heritage* Conservation offers new avenues for finding out about objects and hence the world around us – for instance, analysis of the blue pigments in paintings, which are derived from the Levant trade, remind us that global commerce is not all that new a phenomenon. It also has very specific importance: if the UK is seeking to demonstrate and share the wealth of its collections, then it had better be seen to be looking after them. 'Giving dignity' to the differences to which James Purnell referred requires demonstrating that objects are adequately cared for in ways that reflect the cultures from which they come.
· *The UK as a centre of cultural professionalism* As the balance of the global economy changes and the dominance of the USA and the West is challenged by economies like India and China, it is not just banking and commerce that will keep Britain a G8 country, but also the capacity to export skills and knowledge.

The conservation sector is well ahead of the game in doing this. Many conservators work closely with colleagues in other countries and through membership of organisations like the International Institute for Conservation (IIC) and the International Council of Museums (ICOM), and, notably for its Conservation Committee, participate in global professional networks. Objects are sent from abroad to undergo treatment in the UK; at Portsmouth docks, for instance, you will see not only the *Mary Rose*, but also a trireme from Greece. In the private sector, practices like Plowden & Smith and Hardman's, the stained-glass specialists in Birmingham, take commissions from all over the world.

Education

More than half – 57 per cent – of all the conservation training available in Europe takes place in the UK's HEIs.[54] Large numbers of foreign students come to the UK because it is recognised as having the leading centres of conservation training, like the UCL Institute of Archaeology, the TCC, the Hamilton Kerr and the University of Northumbria in the domain of painting conservation, West Dean in Sussex (in furniture, clocks, ceramics, metalwork and book conservation), and Camberwell in London (paper and book conservation). For example, approximately half of the TCC's students are from abroad. Museum professionals from the British Museum working in Ethiopia have also identified conservation as a pressing need in the country's museums workforce, and training exchanges have begun. However, if the government is serious about marketing UK education abroad and, as James Purnell stated, 'sharing our expertise' with Africa and Asia – the areas to which the World Collections Programme is devoted – then the infrastructure of the UK's own conservation education and expertise must be maintained.[55]

International exchange

There is a healthy tradition of international knowledge transfer within the sector. In February 2007 arms and armour conservators from the Royal Armouries in Leeds and the Wallace Collection in London travelled to Rajasthan in India to participate in a two-day conference called 'The Future of Indian Arms and Armour Collections: Their Study and Conservation'. They learned traditional methods used to conserve weaponry and, in particular, traditional techniques that used 'a minimum of the tooling that Western European craftsmen seem to find so essential' but nevertheless achieved high quality results. In fact, the conservators purchased equipment for use in museum-handling in the UK, and are experimenting with traditional media and techniques in the conservation of the collections they care for here. In exchange, Indian conservators will make a reciprocal visit to gain experience of working in the conservation departments of some of the UK's leading institutions.[56]

Encouraging tourism

Conservation is central to the upkeep of many of the objects and buildings that attract tourists to Britain. Figures of the Office for National Statistics show that every year some 85 per cent of overseas visitors to the UK – which equates to about 28 million people – say that they come here for our heritage, museums and galleries.[57] Furthermore, of the top ten most visited attractions in the UK, conservation plays a vital role in the sustenance of nine, be it in the treatments undertaken on paintings, or on the fabric of the White Tower at the Tower of London, currently under wraps and printed with the message 'Giving the White Tower the care it deserves' (photo 8).[58]

The tourism generated by culture and heritage is also important in economic terms. Overall, tourism is a vital part of our economy. Every year £85 billion is spent on tourism, which is directly responsible for 1.4 million jobs.[59] Without conservation, we could not sustain many of the attractions for which people come to the UK and, ultimately, the economic benefit that follows.

As well as dealing with the wear and tear that results from tourism, the cause of conservation can also benefit from the attention that it brings. A contributor to the Getty Conservation Institute report mentioned earlier argued that 'without heritage tourism, many sites and artefacts would be less able to fend off development and other pressures'.[60] Certainly, the prestige and global recognition that being listed by Unesco as a World Heritage Site can bring to an area or site contributes to both its tourist appeal and the value that is placed on caring for it.

6 A crisis for conservation education?

While the threat of losing conservation education will impact on the cultural sector and policy makers alike, responsibility for that threat in the first place cannot be laid solely at the door of either politicians or cultural leaders, universities or, for that matter, of conservators themselves. In like manner, the action that must be taken to avoid the threat will involve all these groups, individually and in partnership.

One of the barriers to effective partnership is the confusion and misunderstanding that exist in relation to the role of the conservator. According to two leading academics in the sector, conservation is 'a young discipline... in the last century, it has been struggling to define its own identity in response to the rapid changes that have shaped the world'.[61] This has repercussions at policy level: as the 2006 House of Lords Science and Technology Committee noted, 'at the moment, the sector is fragmented and widely dispersed. There are many players: DCMS and its agencies, the devolved administrations, the National Museums and Galleries, universities, the Museums, Libraries and Archives Council (MLA), Research Councils... private sponsors and the charitable sector.'[62]

The problem is that, if conservators are to lead in developing the ethos of caring for the material world, they can only do so if there is a good public understanding of their role. For that to happen, the issues facing conservation need to be addressed, and the conservation sector will need support from both government and the cultural professions. To understand how to tackle the problems, we need to understand how they have arisen in the first place.

Picking up the pieces: the challenges faced by the conservation sector

At first glance, the threat to conservation education – and hence conservation – seems to have come about because current models of providing training for conservators appear unsustainable within the higher education system unless integrated as part of a larger whole, like a fine art or archaeology department, which themselves face stiff competition for resources with other departments. As we have seen, this is at heart a financial problem and, at the moment, there would appear to be no clear-cut solution. Heritage and cultural institutions are willing where possible to contribute to training in the sector, but the burden of training cannot be picked up by institutions that have neither the time nor the funding and, after all, are not education providers.

Fundamentally, however, the problems faced by conservation education are also faced by conservation more broadly and relate to the underlying causes of the financial problems rather than to the financial problems themselves. If more students enrolled on conservation courses, then the income from fees would go up – but it is not as straightforward as that because greater student numbers will also require the commitment of greater resources (space, staffing, equipment) to be able to teach the additional students and maintain excellence. If the public profile of conservation was higher, then research grants, corporate partnerships and sponsorship would be easier to attract, enabling conservation programmes to fit better within the economic model applied by universities. If conservation were seen as figuring more significantly in the public interest, then it would be easier for budget-holders in cultural and heritage institutions to allocate funding to conservation and conservation training.

Conservators and cultural leaders must raise the profile of conservation and demonstrate the value that it adds to society, and to do this they must confront three issues:

· misconceptions of conservation

- the low professional standing of conservation within the culture and heritage sector
- lack of representation at policy level

Misconceptions of conservation

In 2008 a trailer on British TV announced a forthcoming property show. A couple was seen puzzling over whether or not to buy a house that was a listed building. They were tempted, but thought they might also want to make some alterations. At this point, the listed building surveyor came in, shook his head and said they couldn't. Time for the show's miracle-working hostess to come in and sort things out...

This snippet of popular culture reveals much about perceptions of conservation. The listing of the building *could* have been presented as a huge attraction to the house. But it wasn't. Conservation is often stereotyped as nit-picking and blinkered. It can suffer from an image problem, and this has an impact at a number of levels.

High profile news pieces like the restoration of a priceless violin accidentally smashed by a musician bring the sector to public attention. But they are a mixed blessing for the conservator.[63] The prevalence of such stories masks the bulk of conservation work that goes on. Highly effective conservation is often *un*seen. The theme that strings the stories of Djenné's mosque and Lorenzetti's Siena together is the *prevention* of damage. This is where the conservation sector adds real value, but while the smashing of a single vase hits international headlines, thousands of dehumidifiers hum unnoticed in the corners of our museums, galleries and stately homes, and collection care is seen merely as routine activity – put another way, '*The Hay Wain* isn't degrading' is never going to be a headline. The challenge will be in making a public virtue out of the *prevention* of damage, and out of the *maintenance* of the public sphere, in much the same way as caring for the walls of Djenné is seen as a duty, and as a source of pride and pleasure.

The low professional standing within the cultural and heritage sectors

Few conservators occupy high-level management posts in cultural and heritage organisations, and it is rare that conservators play as prominent a public role around high profile exhibitions as their curatorial colleagues.

From the professional perspective, it is very often the conservator's job to point out the practical parameters that can limit the ambitions of curators in museums and heritage. At the extremes, the age-old distinction of mind and matter, brain and brawn, and art and craft can kick in: the curator is perceived as dealing with the intellectual, the conservator merely with the physical. One conservator interviewed for this research observed that, in museums, the profession can be seen as 'brown-coated serfdom' or a 'service industry' for the aristocracy of curators and exhibition organisers.[64]

As conservation has matured as a discipline, it has more than demonstrated its intellectual merit, and curatorial opinions like the one above are the exception rather than the rule. However, vestiges of inferiority remain. Typically, the pay of conservators is 2 per cent below that of university technicians at entry level, but 20 per cent below at senior level and, when increases in the cost of living are taken into account, the growth in conservators' pay over the past 15 years has left them 'much less well-off than their peers in similar roles' in other sectors.[65] In one case, Icon came across a conservator graded as a cleaner due to a bureaucratic misconception of what he actually did.[66] Similarly, it is only recently that collections care has been factored into the MLA's Renaissance in the Regions scheme.

In the past, conservation has not always been championed by leaders in the cultural sector. In a 2002 roundtable of some of the world's leading museum directors, one of the most senior American professionals expressed his concern about what he saw as being the complexity and alchemy of conservation:

I would be very hesitant to bring too much specificity, too many details about the whole cookery of conservation to the public. I feel about it I guess the same way the medical profession would about trying to explain in great detail all of the procedures in a difficult surgical intervention. And in terms of public trust... I wonder if we aren't dealing with something too difficult, too complex. I have seen many a curator utterly bemused... and not even understanding what some of the treatment is they are approving... I don't think the public has any business looking at what the conservator is doing.

However, as a fellow participant responded, 'public trust demands the authenticity of the experience that is being produced... conservation is part of that'.[67]

The conservator-curator

When the British Museum's exhibition 'Hadrian: Empire and Conflict' opened in 2008, the kernel of its appeal was a reinterpretation of the philosopher-emperor. Images and statues of Hadrian show him either appearing in military garb, or cutting a more Hellenic dash in a toga.

One such statue had stood in the British Museum for the last century and a half. Until, that is, conservators examining the material of the statue recognised that the proportions of the head and arms did not match the body. Removing layers of plaster, they revealed that the image of Hadrian in the statue was actually a Victorian construct, a cut and paste of antique statues.

Conservation of the statue did more than provide curators with new information about the Roman image of Hadrian. It also offered an unexpected insight into the Victorian view of history. Such reinterpretation was only possible through the work of the conservator in combining the management of the material of the statue with an intellectual understanding of its form, history and function.[68]

Lack of representation at policy level

Despite the contributions that the sector makes, conservation is under-represented in policy making. In all sectors, conservators rely on the public cultural and heritage sector for either employment or business, and – through major museums, non-departmental public bodies like English Heritage and non-governmental organisations – representation. Furthermore, because there are distinct disciplines of conservation there is also a natural diversity within the sector itself. Different disciplines within conservation have developed their own specialisms and costs. Textile conservators, for instance, need to train in order to develop skills in handling materials specific to their work. Alongside the theoretical awareness of chemicals and materials common to all conservators, painting conservators have to understand painterly production and art history when training for their field, and also require space and equipment to manage easel paintings that are often quite large and potentially burdensome in terms of insurance. Elsewhere, stained-glass conservators – whose work is integral to maintaining many of the great buildings of the UK, from the Palaces of Westminster to cathedrals like York Minster – develop sophisticated craft skills in making glass in addition to learning conservation. Such diversity compounds the lack of coherence and unity created by the division between the private sector, the public sector and HEIs. Although independence is important at sectoral level because it clarifies responsibilities and provides an internal structure to the profession, at policy level it is a weakness.

As it stands, there is very little governmental policy that relates directly to conservation. For instance, the white paper *Heritage Protection for the 21st Century* deals only with the built environment. When conservation can add so much and the material world is so important to our public realm, this is a startling omission.

The House of Lords Select Committee and the Science and Heritage Programme

When in 2006 the House of Lords Science and Technology Committee stressed the level of threat that the neglect of conservation holds for the UK's cultural heritage, it also noted that: 'the Department for Culture, Media and Sport has hitherto failed to grasp the scale of this threat – indeed, it probably does not know it exists'. It recommended that DCMS

Photo 1 Ceremonial repair of the temple at Djenné, source:
www.visitgaomali.com/DjenneRemudding1.JPG

Photo 2 Conservation and display at the SS *Great Britain*, image courtesy of the SS Great Britain Trust, all other rights reserved

Photo 3 Conservation and display at the SS *Great Britain*, image courtesy of the SS Great Britain Trust, all other rights reserved

Photo 4 'Conservation in Focus' at the British Museum, © Trustees of the British Museum

Photo 5 The conserved painted linen scenery at Normansfield Hospital, reproduced courtesy of the Langdown Centre Trust

Photo 6 Members of the Maori community welcoming visitors to Hinemihi, June 2003, image courtesy of Dean Sully

Photo 7 UCL conservation students conducting a physical survey of Hinemihi, June 2003, image courtesy of Dean Sully

Photo 8 Conservation of the White Tower, © Historic Royal Palaces

Photo 9 Volunteering at Tyntesfield, image courtesy of the National Trust

should 'review its departmental objectives in light of the Government's policy on sustainability' and, in particular that 'the Department add to its objectives an explicit reference to the need to conserve our cultural heritage for the benefit of future as well as existing communities'.[69]

In response to the Committee's report, the Arts and Humanities Research Council and the Engineering and Physical Sciences Research Council collaborated to fund the Science and Heritage Programme. Its stated aims are to:

- *build capacity through opportunities for collaboration among disciplines ranging from arts and humanities to science, engineering and technology and*
- *to fund interdisciplinary research and support training of young researchers*[70]

The principle underlying the programme is to increase the knowledge by which we can manage our heritage in the twenty-first century, addressing new and emergent needs like climate change and the sustainability of materials.

The programme also sets an agenda for collaboration. It makes a clear connection between heritage and science, and therefore sets a paradigm for the sort of cross-sectoral support and funding that will help conservation meet the challenges of the new century and carry the value of the sector's innovation into other areas like energy and climate change, and science and industry.

Winning support

For the conservation sector to survive and flourish, support is needed at both policy and funding level in the cultural and education sectors. The challenge for conservators will be in winning that support in the context of multiple and competing claims from the cultural sector and beyond.

In budgetary terms, DCMS is the smallest of government departments, and within it culture must be balanced with media and sport. To win support for conservation, leaders at the top of the cultural and heritage sector will have to make their case even more strongly than before – especially in a time of economic downturn. The same applies within institutions and HEIs, where budgets have to be balanced between different needs and departments.

Part of the answer lies in demonstrating the many different values conservation can add. Although conservation might seem cost-intensive in financial terms, it reaps rewards in terms of the value it generates. Consequently, while part of the solution to the challenges the sector faces will be increased funding and support, part will also be in making the costs of conservation and conservation education more acceptable by increasing the store that is placed upon them. If the future of conservation is to be subject to market forces, then that market must be given adequate information on which to make judgements, be it from the perspective of allocating public budgets, or of private individuals spending their own money. To do this, conservators must build wider awareness of the sector's importance, and connect their work to wider concerns.

7 Conservation and the wider world

Over the last quarter of a century culture has moved from the margins of people's concerns to being central to issues such as the creative economy, tourism, identity and the relationships between nations. In turn the heritage sector has become recognised as being more important. This means two things for conservation. First, it sets a context in which the values of conservation – care, prevention and treatment – have wider relevance within public life (see boxes 3, 4 and 5). Second, it means that the practices and attitudes of conservation, in common with many other disciplines, will have to adapt to changes in the world around it.

The sociologist Zygmunt Bauman has described the new, interconnected world as 'liquid modernity', defined by constant change and the questioning of the conventional.[71] As we seek to make sense of this world, our means of doing so seem increasingly outmoded.[72] New communication technologies and migration have led to much greater exchange and interaction between societies and peoples, but this has led us to question our identity, as we struggle to make sense of what it now means to be 'British' or 'French', a Londoner or a Parisian. To counteract this, we turn to culture and heritage to get a grip on the world around us: Prime Minister Gordon Brown, for instance, welcomes the idea of a 'Museum of Britishness' and governments around the world are promoting cultural exchange as never before.

The problem is that, in turning to culture and heritage for answers, politicians and others rarely take into account the full complexity of that context. To provide a better sense of that complexity, we can look at the story of the film *300*, released in early 2007.

Lessons of 300

In 2007 the film 300, *which was based on a successful US graphic novel, grossed nearly US$71 million in its first weekend in the USA; by mid-May, worldwide takings amounted to some US$440 million.*[73] *However,* 300 *also generated an international response that the producers would not have hoped for. It told the story of the Battle of Thermopylae in conventional Hollywood terms: the Spartans were heroes, and the Persians the baddies.*

*In the current climate of international relations, the depiction of Persians as barbarian and sybaritic in an American film proved incendiary. In the USA, bloggers from Iranian diaspora communities quickly expressed their anger. One wrote that 'not only does it [*300*] give the wrong outcomes to battles, it grossly misrepresents the Persians and their civilization… It is unfortunate that very few curriculums in the USA cover world history and it is very easy to misdirect the general public on historical facts.'*[74] *This and similar protests quickly began to feature on global news websites,*[75] *and soon came to the attention of politicians; according to Javad Shamaqdari, a cultural adviser to Iran's President Ahmadinejad, the film was 'plundering Iran's historic past and insulting this civilization'.*[76] *Some protesters rigged Google's search engine so that searches for '*300*' led not to the film's official site, but to another that platformed Iranian culture and heritage, linking to museums around the world with Persian collections. They recognised the importance of cultural artefacts in combatting what they saw as being the ill-effects of popular culture.*

300 *is a demonstration of many of the recent changes that now affect culture and heritage and, hence, conservation. First, it underlines the importance of individual action, and how quickly participative technologies can be used to escalate its effect. It also demonstrates how diaspora and migration coupled with mass communication have brought people of different viewpoints together as never before. And it shows how culture is becoming more important to a range of policy agenda as both a space in which conflict is felt, and as something to which people can turn to assuage disagreement.*[77]

The trends brought out in the story of *300* are deeply interconnected and are shaping the world in ways that will require change of conservation and many sectors besides.

The shift to the individual

In many areas of life we have seen a shift from the generalised to the individual. In the workplace, Fordist models of command and control have given way to more individualised patterns of working.[78] As consumers, we want to personalise the goods we buy – the new Fiat 500 has half a million individual design combinations for the customer to choose from. In our daily lives, we are moving from producer-determined to consumer-led services; we expect local government to provide public services that meet our specific, rather than generalised, needs.[79]

This amounts to a revolution in the way we think of providers of goods and services: because we want to exert our own choice, we seem to trust professionals and experts less. From GM foods to the judgements of critics in papers, our relationship with the expert has changed. Scientists assure us that certain foods are safe, but many refuse to eat them; and although critics and academics alike tore *The Da Vinci Code* to shreds, millions bought it, loved it, believed it and watched the film.[80] Experts are not irrelevant, but their relationship with the public is changing to become more consultative than didactic: 'a move away from a deferential culture to one in which an informed public is more likely to challenge and critique institutions and professions'.[81] This has radical implications for the way that public services are delivered. It also has radical implications for the relationship between the citizen and the state; between the public and the professional; and in terms of culture and heritage, between the individual and cultural institutions and professionals; and, indeed, for the idea of who determines what . constitutes culture and heritage in the first place.

The need to accommodate individual preference is affecting museums and other cultural institutions. At Tate Britain, for example, visitors can pick up leaflets that map paths around the galleries not just according to curatorial interpretation, but also according to moods and feelings. There is the 'First date' tour and – for those coming from a less upbeat perspective – the 'I've just split up' tour as well. There is also a completely blank leaflet that enables visitors to create their own tour according to their mood, and leave it for others to follow.[82]

Such enterprise in the cultural and heritage sector is important because, more widely, the importance of individual decisions is also influencing policy making. The UK Government's Strategy Unit and the Home Office are both investigating the politics of public behaviour, recognising that individual decisions and behaviours dictate government's ability to effect change.[83] In the USA and, according to Shadow Chancellor George Osborne, here as well, the politics of 'nudging' – providing parameters within which policy ends are reached by guiding individual choice without compromising its integrity – will become more prevalent as governments seek to prompt public choices in what Osborne calls 'the post-bureaucratic age'.[84]

Box 3

The relevance of conservation: reflecting individual values
As interest in such high profile pieces as the Fitzwilliam's Qing vases demonstrates, the public do respect the skill of the conservator. In other sectors, the changing role of the expert is better understood as a process of involving the public more in decision making rather than as a diminution of skills and training. This has created an expectation of personalisation and, because conservation deals with the preservation of values, and these are held by individuals, it is likely to create new expectations of the sector.

This will challenge conservators because, as our communities become more and more complex, conservation will have to reflect more and more individual values. However, it also opens new potential: by encouraging the public to take part in caring for the material world, conservators can create new ways in which people can shape and relate to the public realm. Conservators can play a vital role in encouraging and facilitating new patterns of public behaviour around caring for the material world.

An increased will to participate

'Collaboration is the new revolution' read an editorial headline in the *Guardian* in August 2008.[85] Participation and collaboration connect with the rise of the individual and our changing relationship to expertise: in fact, it is expertise that provides the logic that binds mass collaboration together. As the writer on innovation and creativity Charles Leadbeater observes, 'an amateur did not write *A Brief History of Time* – but in the future, aspects of astronomy will depend on dedicated amateurs working in tandem with professionals motivated by a shared sense of excitement about exploring the universe'.[86] This is because the interest in astronomy and the overwhelming amount of material to be studied combines with the vastly enhanced means by which to collaborate.

The *Guardian* editorial observed, 'the cooperative spirit that infused the open source movement is now in expansive mood, as people and corporations collaborate on music, science, architecture, knowledge, video sites such as YouTube, and social networks, including MySpace, Facebook and Bebo'.[87] The mass uptake of social software is generating new attitudes, behaviours and expectations. It is also driving a diversification of interests. For example, the photo-sharing website Flickr enables niche interests to be showcased and shared, and users have generated groups around specific types of image or styles of photography. It is not necessarily that these interests are significant in themselves, but, as a whole, the movement allows people to focus on their particular interests, and also to generate peer groups around just about anything they want.[88]

Box 4   **The relevance of conservation: providing the chance to engage**
Like all other sectors, conservation will have to respond to these changes. As the importance of culture and heritage becomes

more apparent, so people will want to participate and be involved in conservation.

This contains inherent risk, as any professional conservator who has had to undo 'restorative' work carried out without professional supervision and training will tell you. But the future must be one of managing that risk and communicating the value of conservation. Conservators can offer cultural institutions and cultural policy makers the chance to develop opportunities for people to engage with and shape their culture and heritage. Increased participation will also mean that conservation will have to take account of diverse heritages and competing claims for attention. Conservation is a means of championing interests and of making statements about what is worth keeping (or not).

The effects of mass travel, migration and diaspora

The growth of diaspora communities, the ease with which people can travel overseas and the intensified flow of information enabled by global communication media mean that we encounter a far greater diversity of cultures than ever before. Culture is a space in which we relate to one another and this has changed the role and expectations placed on institutions in the cultural and heritage sector. More than half (57 per cent) of the UK public agree that immigrants make Britain more open to new ideas and cultures.[89] Reflecting this, the understanding of heritage and cultural provision in the UK has shifted to reinforce the idea of presenting different heritages and different cultures. Museums and other heritage organisations now play a vital role in the wider agenda of inclusion. The objects in institutions help us come to terms with the values of others, and they are also important in providing diaspora communities with the opportunity both to link back to their traditions and to communicate their beliefs and world views.

Culture, however, is not always a 'safe space'; it can also be the flashpoint for disagreement. It is one of the ways that we sense difference and, because it is so closely linked to identity, it is particularly sensitive.[90] When different values are brought into close proximity, disagreements are bound to emerge. *300* aroused such anger because it was a mainstream film; the protest was effective because of people's capacity to respond to it as individuals and to publish their opinions freely and easily. As cultural production moves into the hands of the many, such instances are likely to multiply. Similarly, it must be borne in mind that, as well as providing a means of communicating values, cultural and heritage forms in museums and other institutions can also spotlight difference.

Box 5   **The relevance of conservation: communicating different world views**

More and more people will come into contact with the cultural and heritage artefacts that comprise the UK's collections. Equally, UK collections will have to expand to include many different kinds of objects to reflect a changing visitor population and the need to incorporate diverse viewpoints about the objects that our institutions look after. As this happens, demonstrating that they are cared for in appropriate ways that reflect the cultures that they represent, and including those communities in their interpretation and presentation, will be crucial.

Equally, different cultures will bring new ideas of care, and introduce new values to conservation. Many conservators are already working to include these, and this offers cultural policy makers the opportunity to include these values in cultural provision, and also to develop the workforce in ways that reflect authentic practices of care through which they can be communicated. Furthermore, as the work done at Hinemihi exemplifies, because conservation relates to the awareness of materiality it is also a powerful means of communicating different world views and approaches to the material world.

8 Projecting a spectrum of conservation

How society responds to the changing role of culture outlined in the previous chapter will be a central question of government in the early twenty-first century. Conservation can help answer it. Generally, the role of the cultural professional is evolving and perceptions of cultural provision are changing from the position of holding knowledge to acting as a guide, interpreter and enabler of all the knowledge and opinion bound up in the audiences participating in culture and heritage.[91] It is not that professional expertise is irrelevant – far from it – rather, it is integral to sparking the interest of others, enabling culture and heritage to reflect the multiple values that those engaging with it will bring, and reflecting those values back to the public.

The Deliberately Concealed Garments Project

Run by the Textile Conservation Centre, the Deliberately Concealed Garments Project is an example of mass-collaboration, promulgated and guided by experts. It also makes conservation advice readily available. From the Middle Ages there was a tradition in Britain in which garments and other objects associated with either superstition or personal stories were hidden in the fabric of buildings. Many have subsequently been discovered.

Aware of the rich heritage hidden in this tradition, researchers at the TCC sought to develop a way of accessing it. The many garments and objects hidden or buried around the country would reveal much about our material history and the beliefs and attitudes that caused them to be hidden. However, the task of finding – let alone documenting – it would be way beyond the limited resources of the Centre.

The TCC's solution was to launch a website on which people could find information about objects that had been uncovered, and contribute the knowledge gathered to a centralised pool. This created a research tool driven by mass collaboration. It also opens the ideas and values of conservation to the public, making it clear that everyday decisions can have an impact on the wider heritage of the nation. [92]

A spectrum of conservation

Schemes like the Deliberately Concealed Garments Project make an active contribution to the renegotiation and public shaping of our heritage. They draw on the public's knowledge, engage the public in conservation, and provide the basis for a groundshift in how we engage with our heritage and the links between everyday care and the idea of conservation.

A spectrum runs from the high-level practice of skilled, professional experts, through to the more everyday decisions that we make in our daily lives (figure 2). Ultimately, the decisions made at the most technically adept levels of the sector in the most highly professional contexts are based on the same values as those on which we all base our decisions, whether it be not to leave a photograph we like in the sun, or – in more everyday terms – not to drop litter on the street.

Figure 2 **The spectrum of conservation**

High levels of training

A public active in conservation

Practices of conservation

Complex and professional treatment and interventions

Everyday decisions

Conservation's appeal offers new spaces in which to satisfy a growing public will to participate. At a time at which policy makers are seeking to reflect public choice in the public realm, and have to rely more on public choice to meet many of the challenges that we face, conservation can draw on public interest and the public will to engage. It can provide an avenue by which to help people express their own values, and take an active role in championing and protecting the ideas and practices with which they identify. This is why conservation has particular relevance to issues like integration and cohesion.

Rob Dulstone, video-game restorer

In the Guardian's *weekend supplement there is a weekly column which asks members of the public 'Are you happy?'. One such interviewee was a former City worker, called Rob Dulstone. Having been made redundant, Rob said that he 'took the opportunity to explore a lifestyle that brought him more happiness'. Now, he works part-time in investment banking and part-time restoring video games.*

'I'm not a massive player,' says Rob, 'I get my kicks from problem-solving – seeing how these things tick rather than how long I can play them.' He also appreciates the value that his restoration work gives to his clients: 'people have that memory – that feeling they can pin back to when they first got their hands on a machine. That sense of nostalgia is awakened.'

Rob's work exemplifies the value of conservation. It is miles away from the complex work of many heritage and conservation professionals, treating major objects like Holbein's The Ambassadors *or the Crown Jewels. However, it is based on the same values: what people find important and what connects to their sense of identity. In pursuing his personal interests, Rob – like many others who undertake similar hobbies or even just take the time to volunteer – is part of the wider ethos of conservation that can energise the public sphere. Rob deals directly with people's memories. Thinking of work like his in the same terms as we do the complex work in our institutions, we can take a step towards building a sense of active care of our material world.*[93]

Building from an interest in conservation and activity like that of Rob, described in the case study above, the potential of conservation becomes apparent. There is much to be learned from the Finnish concept of *talkoot*.

Talkoot

Talkoot *(singular:* talkoo*) form part of a Finnish practice in which people within a community come together to achieve a common goal. Traditionally, communities are dispersed, with families living on farmsteads often many miles apart. In order to achieve larger ambitions, for example building a barn or another large structure, it was therefore necessary to come together.*

Talkoot *have remained a part of Finnish life and fulfil a quasi-ritualistic function. They have evolved into a voluntary and unpaid gathering of community members to achieve something for the good of the group. Not turning up or not pulling your weight is seen as lack of contribution to the community, and hence lead to a loss of image or status.*[94]

There are parallels between the idea of a talkoo *and the idea of conservation. Both are about the sustenance and nurture of the public realm and community. How might the idea of conservation be reinforced by* talkoo-*like gatherings in the UK?*

In a recent Demos pamphlet, Liam Byrne, then Minister of State for Borders and Immigration, proposed a 'National Day to celebrate what we like best about our country'.[95] *The Minister wrote about plenty of suggestions made to him by members of the public as to how this should be celebrated, but he also acknowledged the concern that had been expressed. There is the risk that a 'Britain Day' could be retrospective or alienating.*[96]

What if the emphasis was shifted from the reinforcement of pre-ordained values to creation and care? Applying the model of a talkoo, *members of the public could work with trained conservators to identify and care for objects, buildings – or even ideas – they value. Doing so would help people to articulate their own values, learn about the values of the past and of other cultures, and create new values reflected in the material world in which they live. Collectively, these would amount to a powerful moment of celebration of the UK in a way that reconnects people with the material world.*

9 Building capital from interest

Start with people

In 2006 98 per cent of adults saw at least one heritage programme on television and, within that, 20 per cent saw at least 99 programmes.[97] In 2003 *Restoration*, which dealt specifically with the conservation of buildings of historic and heritage interest, is reported to have attracted an average of 3.5 million viewers per episode, thus demonstrating the wide appeal of conservation.[98]

> **Meet the Mummies: the public interest in conservation**
>
> *At Birmingham Museums and Art Gallery, the conservation department undertook work on the Egyptian collections while the galleries were closed for refurbishment. The conservators decided to take the opportunity to offer the general public a chance to look at the mummies and other Egyptian material at close quarters and hosted an open day as part of Museums and Galleries month in May 2008.*
>
> *Small groups were invited into the studios to look at the objects and ask questions of conservation staff. They could handle objects, and look at X-rays that revealed what the conservators were doing and what information they had found out. The event proved so successful that the conservation team had to provide another day's activities to meet demand.*

What *Restoration* and the like *fail* to do is demonstrate the way that conservation is essential to the maintenance of our public realm. Public interest is the starting point from which professionals can develop awareness of the value and importance of caring for the material world. There are many instances in which this is under way. As in the example from Birmingham, above, they show that conservation is as much about discovering more about objects as it is about looking after them. Elsewhere conservators demonstrate how their world can play an active role in the present.

Caring for the political world

On Cromwell Green, in front of the UK's Houses of Parliament, stands Hamo Thronycroft's 1897 statue of Oliver Cromwell. In August 2008 conservation work on it began: the surface is being cleaned, and will then be repatinated to return it to a state as close as possible to the one in which it is presumed to have been conceived. [99]

The treatment is to prepare the statue for September 2009, the 350th anniversary of Cromwell's death. Conservation is being used as a means of celebrating an icon of British political history and to identify and contribute to the sense of moment around his anniversary.

Furthermore, the work on the Cromwell statue is being relayed on the photo-sharing website Flickr. [100] *The public can see a close-up of the statue's head in which half has been cleaned, while the other half remains caked in grime and black wax. These images are posted by the UK Parliament. This is an example of how new technology can be used to engage the public in the meaning of conservation work, and build anticipation around a project.*

Continuing with professional expertise

In the Flickr page devoted to the Cromwell statue, and other instances like the Deliberately Concealed Garments Project, conservators use new technologies to generate participation in a collective sense of heritage. Conservators can use public interest to communicate and spread the values by which they operate. It is through schemes like this that the 'Long Tail' of conservation and heritage can be accessed. The future of the sector will depend on how conservation professionals can identify new ways of working that marry traditional values with changing contexts and expectations.

The professional values of conservators are the starting point from which the importance of caring for the material world can be developed more widely.

Whose pants won't live forever?

In 1979 Freddie Mercury played a gig to an audience of thousands. For many, Queen's music and the band's image will live on forever. The problem is that their stage clothes will not.

At that gig Freddie wore a pair of bright red, faux-leather trousers. Since then, they have begun to degrade. In 2006 they were sent to the Textile Conservation Centre in Winchester, where conservators were tasked with finding a way of conserving the garment, which required developing a new treatment process. On one level, the team at the TCC was preserving a memory for potentially millions of Queen fans – they also worked on the famous yellow jacket and white trousers that the rock star wore. On another level, they were undertaking important work into the longevity and vulnerability to degradation of modern materials. As one of the conservators put it, 'everyone has this idea that modern fabrics are indestructible... But in fact there are some that are very unstable – and polyurethane happens to be one of them.'

Such innovation in the conservation sector can also take on an international flavour. Since 2002, for instance, conservators at Tate have worked with colleagues from the Getty Conservation Institute in Los Angeles and the National Gallery of Art in Washington DC, as well as polymer chemists from the University of Torino, to examine the conservation issues raised by modern synthetic paints.[101] Painters from Gary Hume and Bridget Riley to Picasso and Andy Warhol have frequently used such paint in their work, and many of their properties are shared with standard household paint. As well as fostering international collaboration and furthering research in the area, such projects could also have significant impact on how we view and use everyday products, from the gloss and matte paint on our walls to the rubber foam used to fill our furniture.

Broadening participation

In responding to change, there are also several areas, central to policy makers' aims and ambitions, in which the conservation sector can develop new practice and methods of working. These are:

- building skills for the future
- encouraging participation and volunteering
- broadening the workforce and providing more entry points to the sector
- accommodating cultural diversity
- innovation

Building skills for the future

In February 2008 the UK's Secretary of State for Culture, Andy Burnham, announced a £70.5 million scheme to create 5,000 cultural and creative apprenticeships a year throughout the country by 2013. The initiative – set out in *Creative Britain: New talents for the new economy* – is run jointly by DCMS and DIUS and hangs on two central proposals: 'more opportunity for young people to develop creative talents at school; and more structured pathways into creative careers'.[102]

Creative Britain pledged:

- to 'conduct research [to assess] that academia is equipping students with the skills they need to make the most effective contribution they can to the creative economy'
- to 'encourage employers and skills providers to set up ground-breaking new innovative places for learning'
- to 'explore the impact of a brand new "academic hub" supporting collaboration between schools, further and higher

education to provide end-to-end development of creative skills for young people aged from 14 through to 25'[103]

More generally, DIUS has outlined its vision for the future of higher education in the UK as being one in which:

- 'Higher Education Institutions work to widen participation beyond young people leaving college or school with good A-levels
- put learners and employers at the heart of their provision
- and strengthen their leading position in international education through excellent teaching and innovative research'[104]

Together, these initiatives set a policy context for conservation education. As we have seen, the UK's centres of conservation education are globally respected and conduct leading international research. Closure of some of these courses would threaten the existence of a coherent sector and the achievement of DIUS' aims. Policy makers must preserve conservation education either by providing funding to cultural institutions in ways that make conservation training conditional, or by supporting HEIs in sustaining a sector that has great value in relation to the public realm.

The policy context is also employment-driven, is centred on the learner, widens participation beyond higher education, and demands collaboration between the education provider and employer institutions. Conservators must take the opportunity to position the sector at the forefront of areas in which the government is currently trying to innovate.

Encouraging participation and volunteering

An increased appetite for personalisation and the growing recognition of culture's importance mean that participation will come to define the relationship between the public and cultural providers. Initiatives like the Deliberately Concealed Garments Project provide a starting point for engaging more people in the ethos and practice of conservation. They demonstrate the public appeal of conservation, and the value of incorporating wider points of view in the development of knowledge and understanding in the cultural and heritage sectors. They meet both conservation objectives and the wider political agenda around participation and inclusion and so should be considered in relation to policy beyond the cultural sector.

The National Trust and other organisations like the National Archives already work with volunteers, engaging them in conservation as an active contribution to the social capital that the sector represents. In a recent document, *Private Giving for the Public Good*, the NMDC, MLA and ACE joined forces to argue that 'volunteering should be encouraged at all levels... working with a cultural [or heritage] organisation should become part of an individual's career development, encouraging both creativity and a sense of civic responsibility'.[105]

Such sentiment echoed the recent report on volunteering in the health and social care sectors by Baroness Julia Neuberger, the government's 'volunteering champion', in a recent paper for the Cabinet Office:

the increased role of volunteers in the public services has been controversial among some groups. There is a suspicion among trade unions, for example, that the only motivation for the increased role of volunteers is cost-cutting and job substitution. This should never be the case. The Government must be clear about that. Instead it is about helping to create services that are people centred. Besides, good management that brings about the best outcomes for volunteers, staff and service-users does not come cheaply – this is not a cost cutting measure.[106]

Policy makers are increasingly looking to the third sector and volunteer workforces to provide a means of bringing the public into a closer relationship with the services they consume, and to give people the opportunity to engage in public life. Some conservators already work with volunteers. As the concept of culture and heritage widens to include more diverse backgrounds and opinions, volunteering will provide conservation professionals with a means of accessing and responding to greater demand on their expertise and services.

The number of vital and urgent conservation tasks far outnumbers the conservators available to fulfil them – tasks like documentation, storage and preventive work. Volunteering will not only help conservators to get things done, but also provide a route by which the public can develop an interest in conservation and possibly be encouraged to pursue a career in the sector.

Restoring Tyntesfield

Tyntesfield is a National Trust property near Bristol. It is one of the finest Victorian Gothic Revival buildings in the country and was purchased in 2002 after a public fund-raising campaign to ensure that it would be accessible to the public. The appeal was so successful that it raised £8.2 million in just 100 days and, with the help of what was then the largest single grant by the National Heritage Memorial Fund of £17.2 million and an additional £20 million from the HLF, the property was opened to the public within ten weeks of being acquired by the Trust.

The project to conserve aspects of the building is a mammoth undertaking. There are 40 rooms and over 40,000 objects. However, the Trust has decided to take advantage of this Herculean task, both to educate conservators for the future and to engage the public in conservation. Resources allocated to the restoration of the property include an HLF-funded Icon intern in preventive conservation for three years; the Trust is also using Tyntesfield to develop a Skills Passport, which will record the evidence of skills that can be used to support NVQs.[107] Furthermore, any external conservators contracted to work on the property are required to undertake the supervision of volunteers at a range of levels. This does take a deal of the conservators' time but, in the event, the saving on man hours is huge: in 2007, volunteers contributed 40,000 hours of labour, enabling more conservation work to be done.

Volunteering at Tyntesfield plays another role: it is only six miles from Bristol and therefore a wide range of people falls within its catchment area. With this in mind, the Trust has used the conservation of Tyntesfield as an opportunity to reach more diverse audiences. Thus far, 500 people from all walks of life have volunteered to work under the supervision of the Trust's conservators on the project (photo 9).[108] *According to the coordinator of Tyntesfield, 'members of staff skilled in community involvement were appointed as part of the estate team and they continue to work closely with conservation specialists. They are charged with identifying groups or individuals who might benefit from participation and to match skill levels and learning potential to conservation work, providing the essential link between conservators and students.'*[109]

Broadening the workforce and providing more entry points to the sector

One of the advantages of encouraging a wider approach to participation in conservation will be in providing more entry routes into the sector. This will not replace higher education courses, but will complement them. Already, through the framework of professional standards leading to PACR accreditation, the conservation sector is clarifying entry points and the different levels of skills required to practise as a conservator. But there are further opportunities to broaden entry points to the sector, as the initiatives at Tyntesfield demonstrate, where volunteers are given a taster of conservation and graduate conservators are given experience by working alongside the Trust's conservators on more complex tasks. Over and above functional capacity, widening participation in the sector will bring further advantages:

· First, it would provide the starting points from which to progress to higher-level education. Giving people a feel for the sector and a means by which to develop their interest is a means to encourage wider uptake of conservation education at its higher levels. At the moment, many seeking a start in conservation depend either on the support of an employer institution in providing them with training, or on being able to find the time and finance to pursue a postgraduate qualification. This places practical limitations on the degree to which the sector is open to all those who might want to apply.

· Second, formalising different skill levels by developing collaboration between educators and employer institutions to offer different levels of entry point could lighten the burden on many in the sector, helping them take on the vast amount of conservation to be done. Often, conservators feel that many of the tasks that they are asked to carry out do not make the most effective use of their time. Although institutions will have to address the burden that training novice and junior conservators places on their staff, developing junior and volunteer levels of the workforce would help provide the conservation sector with greater structure and, in the long run, help to distinguish the seniority of conservators within the cultural and heritage sector as a whole.

Accommodating cultural diversity

Diversifying the workforce will be important in broadening the participation of different demographic groups in the conservation sector. This would contribute to the diversity of opinion and approach necessary for the sector to develop and flourish, and also impact on the wider politics of diversity and multicultural Britain.

Bringing as many different voices into that process of care as possible will be vital in ensuring that the sector actively represents all the values that make up the UK's culture and heritage today as well as demonstrating the representativeness of the sector's decisions. As the work being undertaken in relation to Hinemihi shows, many in the conservation sector are already doing this. However, through collaboration and public participation, the sector can reach out and include as many different views as possible in conversations around conservation, and inform the professional decisions taken.

Over and above inclusion in the workforce, conservation professionals have time and again proved that their work is a means of discussing artefacts and heritage in terms that are relevant to contemporary debate. Decisions made over conservation treatments are based on negotiations between different values; by bringing values to the fore, conservation professionals can play an important part in how we as a society confront and accommodate difference and the politics of diversity. The symbolism of conservation is becoming increasingly important because the collections of museums and heritage institutions incorporate objects from all over the world. Increased tourism, the growth of diaspora communities and the development of digitised collections mean that collections are seen by more and more people and particularly those from the cultures in which they originate. It is therefore imperative that cultural and heritage organisations in the UK are seen not only to be providing adequate care for them, but also as incorporating the values of those cultures in the caring process.

Innovation

Innovation is central to the thinking of the current government. In his DCMS-commissioned review of 'excellence', Sir Brian McMaster said that 'the desire and ability to innovate and the willingness to take risks is fundamental for any organisation striving to be excellent'.[110] He also recommended that 'innovation and risk-taking be at the centre of the funding and assessment framework for every organisation, large or small'. Similarly, alongside its focus on nurturing talent outside and before higher education, *Creative Britain* also outlines the goal of supporting research and innovation through higher education. Research in cultural and creative subjects drives innovation by developing and funding opportunities for R&D through collaboration between small enterprise and higher education.[111]

The conservation sector is constantly innovating. The techniques developed in research centres in HEIs and cultural and heritage organisations contribute to the UK's international reputation as a centre of excellence and help advance techniques that filter through to the private sector. Innovation will continue to be at the heart of the sector's future, and will be stimulated further by the widened access and participation outlined above.

10 Conclusions and recommendations

The conservation of culture and heritage is rooted in a belief that caring for the material world matters. It matters because it communicates the values of the past, because it allows us to negotiate between values in the present and because it allows us to identify things that we think will be important in the future. An attitude of care towards the world around us produces a range of social goods, from not dropping litter, to looking after our public spaces, to treating the natural environment with respect. Conservation is the discipline from which this idea and ethos springs.

The central recommendations of this pamphlet are that:

- conservators' work should be recognised as **integral not only to the culture and heritage sector but also to social well-being**
- **policy makers, cultural professionals and conservators should collaborate in communicating the importance of caring for the material world and its social benefits to a wider public**
- **conservators should build on existing practice in public engagement and connect their practice to wider agenda**
- **policy makers must support a conservation education sector that has flourished and has an international reputation that is second to none, but is currently under threat**
- **conservators should extend their existing involvement in *social* innovation**. Alongside communicating the importance of care, they can provide a logic that reinforces a less throw-away society, and the need to look after, rather than replace, goods – something which will be essential as we tackle the ills of pollution, climate change and environmental degradation.

It is implicit in these recommendations that attention must be paid to the maintenance and growth of conservation education; that conservation needs to achieve a higher public profile; and that the sector's capacity to attract public support and new funding sources be enhanced. In turn, that means equipping conservators to engage with the public in new ways.

As the chief executive of MLA, Roy Clare, made clear at Icon's 20:20 Vision conference in January 2008, the next Comprehensive Spending Review, due in spring 2009, offers a window of opportunity for conservators to promote the value that the sector adds, and for the wider cultural sector and policy makers to support them. Policy makers, cultural professionals and conservators must work together to promote the appreciation and values of conservation. Together, they can enable the public to become more active in caring for the material world around them.

Specific recommendations

A series of recommendations follows that relate to policy makers, cultural professionals and conservators.

Recommendations for policy makers

· DCMS should take the lead on **a new policy agenda focused on caring for the material world. This should be led by an appointed Adviser who can act as a coordinating voice across different areas of policy and as a public spokesperson who can encourage the public to participate in caring for the material world.**
· The Adviser should lead **a conservation steering group – the Material World Board –** comprising cultural professionals, educators and conservators to devise a strategy for caring for the material world; alongside figures from DCMS, this should include representatives from BERR, CLG, DIUS, DEFRA and DECC, the cultural and heritage sector, and conservators, and should also represent all the UK nations.
· Policy makers should support conservation education. Conservation offers a rare benefit in that it acts as a bridge

between arts and humanities, and the sciences. The conservation steering group **should investigate ways in which conservation education should be supported from a range of funding budgets in the immediate short term,** and should also develop a long-term strategy for higher education and other funding to give conservation education a secure future.

· Funding from centralised governmental and non-governmental sources for specific and larger conservation projects involving a large number of tasks, requiring different skills levels, and on which a number of experienced conservators work, should be conditional on **providing on-the-job training opportunities** for conservators at a range of levels, from entry to postgraduate level. This should particularly be the case in relation to specific areas of training need (the HLF's funding of stained-glass conservation in chapter 4 provides a good example).

· The development of new conservation techniques and the study of different materials have often resulted in innovation. Government should make the most of this and fund conservation techniques on the grounds of innovation as well as the preservation of culture and heritage. A **cross-departmental (DIUS, BERR and DCMS) fund for innovation in conservation** should be established.

· Conservation is important in raising public questions about sustainability: the study of man-made fibres at the TCC, discussed in chapter 9, is a good example. **DEFRA and the new DECC** should work with institutions and educational providers to investigate cross-over with its policy interests.

Recommendations for cultural professionals

· Leaders of the cultural sector should **champion conservation in public, and in funding negotiations** with DCMS, other relevant governmental departments like CLG, DEFRA and DECC, and other funding bodies such as the Arts Councils in England, Scotland, Wales and Northern Ireland. They should see conservation as adding value and new avenues for public engagement rather than as a resource-intensive cost.

- Conservation should be given a **greater profile in exhibitions and displays,** communicating the skills and values of the conservation sector to the museum and gallery-going public. (The British Museum's 'Conservation in Focus' exhibit, described in chapter 3, is a good example of this.)
- **Cultural and heritage institutions should take the opportunity that conservation provides to reflect the practice and world views of living cultures and values.** (Hinemihi, described in chapter 5, is a good example of this.)
- The **public should be engaged in the practice of conservation** in ways that help them express and live their values, and communicate them to others. Museums and other cultural and heritage organisations should use existing museum open days to enable people to 'catalogue' their chosen objects. Professionals would help the public contribute objects to an online database of the nation's culture and heritage, with a space to say why they think it is valuable. This would provide a nationwide picture of objects valued by the public that could stand alongside the collections of museums and other institutions and draw people from different communities and from around the country into communication with each other around objects. It would also have the value of bringing more objects to professional attention.
- **Space should be devoted in every publicly funded museum on at least an annual basis for an object, contributed** *and cared for* **by a member of the public from the surrounding area that represents something of his or her community.** Interpretation panels should relate the process of care to other members of the public, explaining the values that it represents.
- Taking the lead of institutions like the Historic Royal Palaces and others, **conservation should be championed as part of an institution's duty of care**. Cultural institutions should use every opportunity to communicate conservation to the public and, where possible, use technologies or information panels to illustrate the process.

Recommendations for the conservation sector

- The conservation sector should encourage one or more **Conservation Champions to raise the political and public profile of conservation**.
- Following the lead of several in the profession, **all conservators must accept that communicating with the public is part of their role**. In cultural institutions, conservation should be a regular part of the events programme and should focus on making clear the links between the everyday practice of members of the public and the professional work of conservators.
- **Conservators should regularly be involved in public engagement activities.** Taking into account the fact that, as in all professions, some conservators will naturally be more suited to public engagement than others, resources in larger cultural and heritage institutions should be managed accordingly. So, with funding from the government supporting it, resources should be allocated between public engagement and other work so that a certain amount of the conservation staff's time is spent with the public in galleries or with schools.
- Already a feature of some courses, **public engagement and the skills of communicating the values of conservation to the public should be a feature of conservation education**. Equally, conservators of the future should be given the skills by which to relate their practice to wider social agenda and hence the needs of policy makers and the public, as well as maintaining and communicating the sector's own values and ideals.
- As part of the government's initiative of providing five hours of culture to each child each week, schools and other educational institutions should take the opportunity to **invite conservators and student conservators into classes to teach young people the importance of caring for the material world and educate them about objects**, a process that will contribute to building cultural literacy, broaden awareness and future enthusiasm for the sector, and help student conservators develop skills in public engagement.
- Decisions in relation to conservation should be made **taking into account public as well as professional opinion**. In cases that will require the allocation of large amounts of public funds to

conservation treatment, in particular in cases where this might be 'invisible' to the public, **conservation juries should be established in which members of the public are given the full benefit of access to conservators' expertise and conservators can access public opinion in relation to the values brought into the process.** These juries would not be tasked with ultimate decision-making authority, but would be used to prioritise cases for conservation according to public interest, and would recommend how the public might be drawn into the process. The juries would reflect the public's rights, responsibilities and interests in relation to conservation. They would be chaired and managed by trained conservators, who report to, but are independent of, **the Material World Board.**

· Conservators should use new technologies to chart and platform their work. Where appropriate **websites, photo-streaming and blogs should be used to document the work, and explain changes to the object, encouraging, informing and drawing on public discussion.** Comment-boards and blogs should be used to allow the public to ask conservators questions about the work they are doing.

· **Conservators should make greater use of volunteers.** In collaboration with Nature, the Natural History Museum drew on the expertise and manpower of enthusiasts around the country to catalogue the UK's lichen population. This allowed experts in the museum to cover more ground than they previously had been able. As the need to care for the material world becomes more apparent, conservators should do the same. As discussed in chapter 9, at Tyntesfield this has already diversified the audience that the property can reach and it has extended the amount of work that the conservators can undertake.

· In tandem with working in schools and making greater use of volunteers, **conservators and cultural institutions should also provide more opportunities for people to work in conservation.** For higher posts within the profession, higher qualifications should remain, but there should also be opportunities for people to learn and develop qualifications within the profession. Conservators must support this, and **funding bodies and government should look into supporting cultural institutions**

to provide placements for conservators working at different levels to pursue education in employment. Conservators should also take more opportunities to speak in public about their role and the values of the sector, contributing to public debates about the material world and other social issues like littering and recycling. In institutions and HEIs they should work with public relations and public affairs teams to raise awareness of their contribution to the wider issues outlined in this pamphlet and, in particular, the Long Tail of Conservation and the spectrum of conservation. They should also take the opportunity to gain a more public profile by appearing in the media and on television in programmes like the *Antiques Roadshow* and *The Culture Show*, and in relation to wider issues like littering.

Save for the Nation

We also recommend the instigation of a national day for caring for the material world. Initiatives like the Big Draw and the Big Read have brought people together and raised the profile of art and reading. A national conservation day could provide a focus for communities collectively to identify an object, building or even idea of importance and join in its upkeep under the supervision of trained conservators – this could be called Save for the Nation. The effect would be to open people's eyes to the importance of caring for the material world and heritage, provide a means by which people can help care for the public realm, and also provide a point at which the meanings of the things being considered for conservation are discussed and negotiated. Collectively, this would be a significant moment in caring for the material world.

Appendix 1 Methodology

Research for this pamphlet was conducted in the first half of 2008 when 60 people were interviewed to build a picture of the issues facing the sector. Interviewees included representatives of education, employer institutions, the private sector, the student body, government organisations responsible for the sector and cultural policy makers.

The pamphlet has also been informed by discussion at the summit of 12 June 2008, which was convened by **the Textile Conservation Centre with Icon**, around the initial findings of Demos' research. The provocation paper produced for that event can be accessed at the Demos website: www.demos.co.uk/projects/savedforthenation/overview.

Appendix 2 Organisations consulted

Conversations with many individuals in the cultural sector have contributed to the development of this research and we thank those who spared the time to be interviewed. We promised anonymity to those we interviewed, who came from the following organisations:

The Ashmolean Museum, University of Oxford

Birmingham Museums and Art Gallery

The British Library

The British Museum

The Centre for Sustainable Heritage, University College London

The Conservation Unit, Northumbria University

Creative and Cultural Skills

The Department for Culture, Media and Sport (DCMS)

Endangered Heritage Pty Ltd, Australia

English Heritage

The Fitzwilliam Museum, University of Cambridge

The Hamilton Kerr Institute, University of Cambridge

Hampshire Museums and Archives Service

The Heritage Lottery Fund (HLF)

Historic Royal Palaces

Iona Stained Glass

The Institute of Archaeology, University College London

The Institute of Conservation

The International Institute of Conservation of Historic and Artistic Works (IIC)

The Mary Rose Trust

The Museums Association

The Museums, Libraries and Archives Council (MLA)

The Museum of London

The National Archives

The National Gallery

National Historic Ships

The National Trust

Plowden & Smith

Poppy Singer & Annabel Wylie, Freelance Textile Conservators

The Royal College of Art and Victoria & Albert Conservation Course

The Textile Conservation Centre (TCC), University of Southampton

The University of Southampton

The Victoria & Albert Museum (V&A)

Notes

1   See Grose, 'And what big feet you have...', and 'Giant British fertility symbol gets makeover'.

2   Grose, 'And what big feet you have...'.

3   House of Lords Science and Technology Committee, *Science and Heritage*.

4   Mulgan, *Good and Bad Power*.

5   Putnam, 'E pluribus unum'; see also Putnam, *Bowling Alone*.

6   See, for example, House of Commons Environmental Audit Committee, *Environmental Crime*.

7   Sennett, *The Fall of Public Man*.

8   See www.icons.org.uk/theicons/collection/view?mode=list (accessed 12 May 2008).

9   Quoted in House of Lords Science and Technology Committee, *Science and Heritage*.

10 DCMS and Welsh Assembly, *Heritage Protection for the 21st Century*.

11 For fuller discussion of the politics of 'things', see Appadurai, 'Introduction'.

12 Avrami, Mason and de la Torre, *Values and Heritage Conservation*.

13 Sully, *Decolonising Conservation*.

14 House of Lords Science and Technology Committee, *Science and Heritage*.

15 Wilson, *The British Museum*.

16 Quoted in Cuno, *Whose Muse?*

17 In this pamphlet, and for the sake of clarity, English Heritage, Historic Scotland and the National Trust (even though not part of the public sector) are treated as institutional employers of conservators; where differences pertain, this is clarified in the text.

18 Lithgow, 'Developing conservation skills for the future in the National Trust'.

19 Shenton, 'Public engagement with conservation at the British Library'.

20 Demos interview with one of the conservators working on the exhibition, Sep 2008.

21 For further details see 'How do you fix a smashed antique vase?' and the Fitzwilliam Museum's website, www.fitzmuseum.cam.ac.uk/gallery/chinesevases/ (accessed 13 Aug 2008).

22 For further details see Larsen, 'Conservation-restoration education in the light of the European Qualification Framework for Life Long Learning'.

23 For details of the Bologna Process see http://ec.europa.eu/ education/policies/educ/bologna/bologna_en.html (accessed 17 Oct 2008).

24 This is the observation of several of the leading figures interviewed for this research.

25 See www.conservationregister.com/index.asp (accessed 8 Nov 2008).

26 Icon, *Professional Standards in Conservation*.

27 See the statement issued by the TCC announcing its closure at www.textileconservationcentre.soton.ac.uk/newsandevents/ 12_01_closureoftcc.shtml (accessed 15 Aug 2008).

28 This opinion was put forward by an HEI professional interviewed for this research.

29 British Library, *British Library Study*.

30 See Shenton, 'Public engagement with conservation at the British Library'.

31 For further details see www.soton.ac.uk/mediacentre/news/ 2005/may/05_85.shtml and www.langdondowncentre.org.uk/ (accessed 24 Sep 2008).

32 House of Lords Science and Technology Committee, *Science and Heritage*.

33 'Plucked in her prime'.

34 House of Lords Science and Technology Committee, *Science and Heritage*.

35 See, for example, Pye, 'The benefits of access through handling outweigh risks'.

36 See Tait, 'Textile conservation centre stitched up' and associated comments at www.timesonline.co.uk/tol/life_and_style/ court_and_social/article2987329.ece (accessed 15 May 2008).

37 Private correspondence with the Textile Conservation Centre, cited with permission.

38 See www.rca.ac.uk/pages/study/alumni_2079.html (accessed 21 May 2008).

39 Sennett, *The Craftsman*.

40 There are some notable exceptions. Alongside the standing conservation galleries mentioned in detail below, exhibitions have been devoted to conservation. One of the most significant was 'Stop the Rot', at York Castle Museum in 1994, which attracted more than half a million visitors and communicated the impact on heritage objects of damage caused by pollution, climate change, human interference and other phenomena. In 2004 the National Gallery show 'Art in the Making' made use of conservation work to introduce viewers to the artistic process. In 2006 the Fitzwilliam Museum in Cambridge put on 'Mission Impossible?', which was devoted to the skills and profession of conservation.

41 This article is available online at www.wired.com/wired/archive/ 12.10/tail.html (accessed 25 Sep 2006).

42 Anderson, *The Long Tail*.

43 This diagram is adapted from Chris Anderson's models in *The Long Tail*.

44 For fuller discussion of this, see Holden, *Capturing Cultural Value* and *Cultural Value and the Crisis of Legitimacy*.

45 Commission on Cohesion and Integration, *Our Shared Futures*.

46 See www.britishmuseum.org/the_museum/behind_the_scenes/ caring_for_the_collection.aspx (accessed 14 May 2008).

47 For further discussion of Hinemihi, see Burrows, 'Hinemihi and the London Maori community'.

48 Sen, 'How does culture matter?'.

49 For further details of this concept see Bound et al, *Cultural Diplomacy*; Jones, *Building Cultural Literacy*; and Jones, 'Change of culture'.

50 See www.culture.gov.uk/Reference_library/Press_notices/ archive_2008/dcms009_08.htm (accessed 14 May 2008).

51 Miliband, 'New diplomacy'; for further details of the concept of cultural diplomacy see Bound et al *Cultural Diplomacy*.

52 For details of the World Collections Programme, see www.culture.gov.uk/Reference_library/Press_notices/ archive_2008/dcms005_08.htm (accessed 11 May 2008).

53 'Neil MacGregor to chair "World Collections Programme", to share British Cultural Excellence with Africa and Asia'.

54 European Conservation Practitioners License, *The EuroMatrix Heritage*.

55 See www.culture.gov.uk/Reference_library/Press_notices/ archive_2008/dcms005_08.htm (accessed 11 May 2008).

56 For further details see Kitto and Edge, 'The future of Indian arms and armour'.

57 National Museum Directors' Conference, *Values and Vision*; for figures on overseas visitors to the UK, see www.statistics.gov.uk/ CCI/nugget.asp?ID=352 (accessed 30 Sep 2008).

58 See Association of Leading Visitor Attractions, www.alva.org.uk/visitor_statistics/ (accessed 22 May 2008).

59 DCMS, *Winning*.

60 Lowenthal, 'Stewarding the past in a perplexing present'.

61 Pye and Sully, 'Evolving challenges, developing skills'.

62 House of Lords Science and Technology Committee, *Science and Heritage*.

63 See 'How to repair a valuable violin?'.

64 The methodology of the research is described in appendix 1; a list of organisations consulted is provided in appendix 2.

65 Museums Association, *Pay in Museums*.

66 Author's conversation with Alastair MacCapra, then chief executive of Icon.

67 Quoted in Cuno, *Whose Muse?*

68 See Kennedy, 'How Victorian restorers faked the clothes that seemed to show Hadrian's softer side'.

69 House of Lords Science and Technology Committee, *Science and Heritage*.

70 For further details see www.heritagescience.ac.uk/ (accessed 3 Oct 2008).

71 Bauman, *Liquid Modernity*.

72 See, for example, Jones, 'Change of culture'.

73 See www.boxofficemojo.com/movies/?id=300.htm (accessed 15 May 2007).

74 See http://omidmemarian.blogspot.com/ 2007_03_01_archive.html (accessed 15 May 2007).

75 See Joneidi, 'Iranian anger at Hollywood "assault"'.

76 Quoted in Joneidi, 'Iranian anger at Hollywood "assault"'.

77 See also Jones, *Building Cultural Literacy*.

78 Miller and Skidmore, *Disorganisation*.

79 Leadbeater, Bartlett and Gallagher, *Making it Personal*.

80 Lawson, 'Who cares what the reviewers say?'; for comparative examples of the relationship between the public and experts in the domain of science, see Stilgoe, Irwin and Jones, *The Received Wisdom*.

81 Parker et al, *State of Trust*.

82 For fuller discussion, see Jones, 'The new cultural professionals'.

83 Prime Minister's Strategy Unit, *Personal Responsibility and Changing Behaviour*; see also O'Leary, *The Politics of Public Behaviour*.

84 Thaler and Sunstein, *Nudge*; for George Osborne's comments, see Osborne, 'Nudge, nudge, win, win'.

85 'Collaboration is the new revolution'.

86 This and the quote earlier in the paragraph are to be found in Leadbeater, *We-Think*.

87 'Collaboration is the new revolution'.

88 For further discussion, see Shirky, *Here Comes Everybody*.

89 IPSOS MORI, *Public Attitudes to Cohesion and Integration*.

90 Huntington, *The Clash of Civilisations and the Remaking of the World Order*.

91 Jones, 'The new cultural professionals'.

92 For further details see www.concealedgarments.org/ (accessed 24 Sep 2008).

93 Taylor, 'Are you happy?'.

94 I am grateful to Aleksi Neuvonen of Demos Helsinki for drawing my attention to *talkoot*. For details of a project in Finland that uses the concept to tackle climate change, see www.ilmastotalkoot.fi/ (accessed 25 Sep 2008).

95 Byrne, *A More United Kingdom*.

96 Ibid.

97 See www.britarch.ac.uk/research/piccini_2_1.html (accessed 14 Aug 2008).

98 Quoted in Johnston, 'Finalists hit out at Restoration's "silly nostalgia"'.

99 See www.parliament.uk/about/visiting/exhibitions/ cromwell_conservation.cfm (accessed 19 Aug 2008).

100 See www.flickr.com/photos/uk_parliament/2777828772/ (accessed 19 Aug 2008).

101 For further details see www.tate.org.uk/research/tateresearch/ majorprojects/conservation.htm and www.getty.edu/ conservation/science/modpaints/ (accessed 25 Sep 2008).

102 DCMS and DIUS, *Creative Britain*.

103 Ibid.

104 See www.dius.gov.uk/policy/highereducation.html (accessed 19 May 2008).

105 National Museum Directors' Conference, Museums, Libraries and Archives Council and Arts Council England, *Private Giving*

for the Public Good.

106 Neuberger, 'Volunteering in the public services'.

107 Lithgow, 'Developing conservation skills for the future in the National Trust'.

108 For further details see www.nationaltrust.org.uk/main/w-vh/w-visits/w-findaplace/w-tyntesfield/w-tyntesfield-about.htm (accessed 24 Sep 2008).

109 Greenacre, 'Tyntesfield'.

110 McMaster, *Supporting Excellence in the Arts.*

111 DCMS and DIUS, *Creative Britain.*

References

'Collaboration is the new revolution', editorial, *Guardian*, 18 Aug 2008.

'Giant British fertility symbol gets makeover', *Macau Daily Times*, 21 Sep 2008, www.macaudailytimesnews.com/ index.php?option=com_content&task=view&id=16465& Itemid=33 (accessed 16 Oct 2008).

'How do you fix a smashed antique vase?', BBC, 14 Feb 2006, http://news.bbc.co.uk/1/hi/magazine/4708494.stm (accessed 13 Aug 2008).

'How to repair a valuable violin?', BBC, 14 Feb 2008, http://news.bbc.co.uk/1/hi/magazine/7244441.stm (accessed 25 Sep 2008).

'Neil MacGregor to chair "World Collections Programme", to share British Cultural Excellence with Africa and Asia', *Guardian*, 15 Jan 2008, www.culture.gov.uk/reference_library/ media_releases/2138.aspx (accessed 11 Nov 2008).

'Plucked in her prime', *British Archaeology* 90 (2006), www.britarch.ac.uk/BA/ba90/feat2.shtml#allen (accessed 20 May 2008).

Anderson, C, *The Long Tail: How endless choice is creating unlimited demand* (London: Business Books, 2006).

Appadurai, A 'Introduction: commodities and the politics of value' in Appadurai, A, *The Social Life of Things: Commodities in cultural perspective* (Cambridge, Cambridge University Press, 1986).

Avrami, E, Mason, R and de la Torre, M, *Values and Heritage Conservation* (Los Angeles, CA: Getty Conservation Institute, 2000).

Bauman, Z, *Liquid Modernity* (Oxford: Polity Press, 2000).

Bound, K, Briggs, R, Holden, J and Jones, S, *Cultural Diplomacy* (London: Demos, 2007).

British Library, *British Library Study: The need for book conservation in the UK and internationally* (London: British Library, 2004), www.bl.uk/aboutus/stratpolprog/ccare/introduction/training/webconservation.pdf (accessed 12 Nov 2008).

Burrows, K, 'Hinemihi and the London Maori community' in Sully, D, (ed) *Decolonising Conservation: Caring for Maori meeting houses outside New Zealand* (Walnut Creek, CA: Left Coast Press, 2007).

Byrne, L, *A More United Kingdom* (London: Demos, 2008).

Commission on Cohesion and Integration, *Our Shared Futures* (London: Communites and Local Government, 2007).

Cuno, J (ed), *Whose Muse? Art museums and the public trust* (Woodstock: Princeton University Press and Harvard University Art Museums, 2004).

Department for Culture, Media and Sport, *Winning: A tourism strategy for 2012 and beyond* (London: DCMS, 2007).

Department for Culture, Media and Sport and Department for Innovation, Universities & Skills, *Creative Britain: New talents for the new economy* (London: DCMS and DIUS, 2008), www.culture.gov.uk/images/publications/CEPFeb2008.pdf (accesssed 10 Nov 2008).

Department for Culture, Media and Sport and Welsh Assembly, *Heritage Protection for the 21st Century*, Cm 7057 (London: The Stationery Office, 2007).

European Conservation Practitioners License, *The EuroMatrix Heritage: A report on the survey of institutions in conservation education* (Valletta, Malta: Heritage Malta, 2008), http://ecpl-project.heritagemalta.org/publications/Kepha_ECPL_WP2_for matted.pdf (accessed 27 May 2008).

Greenacre, M, 'Tyntesfield: Conservation and the volunteer' in Saunders, D, Townsend, J and Woodcock, S, *Conservation and Access: Contributions to the London Congress*, 15–19 Sep (Dorchester: International Institute for Conservation of Historic and Artistic Works, 2008).

Grose, T, 'And what big feet you have...', *Time Magazine*, 30 Sep 2008, www.time.com/time/world/article/0,8599,1844513,00.html (accessed 16 Oct 2008).

Holden, J, *Capturing Cultural Value* (London: Demos, 2004).

Holden, J, *Cultural Value and the Crisis of Legitimacy* (London: Demos, 2006).

House of Commons Environmental Audit Committee, *Environmental Crime: Fly-tipping, fly-posting, litter, graffiti and noise*, Ninth Report of Session 2003–04, HC 445 (London: The Stationery Office, 2004).

House of Lords Science and Technology Committee, *Science and Heritage*, 9th Report of Session 2005–06, HL Paper 256 (London: The Stationery Office, 2006).

Huntington, S, *The Clash of Civilisations and the Remaking of the World Order* (New York: Simon and Schuster, 1996).

Icon, *Professional Standards in Conservation* (London: Icon, 2007), www.icon.org.uk/images/stories/professional_standards.pdf (accessed 13 May 2008).

IPSOS MORI, *Public Attitudes to Cohesion and Integration* (London: Commission for Integration and Cohesion, Jun 2007), www.integrationandcohesion.org.uk/~/media/assets/www.integr ationandcohesion.org.uk/public_attitudes_towards_cohesion_ and_integration%20pdf.ashx (accessed 8 Nov 2008).

Johnston, J, 'Finalists hit out at Restoration's "silly nostalgia"', *Sunday Herald*, 14 Sep 2003, http://findarticles.com/p/articles/ mi_qn4156/is_20030914/ai_n12584140 (accessed 14 Aug 2008).

Joneidi, M, 'Iranian anger at Hollywood "assault"', 16 Mar 2007, http://news.bbc.co.uk/1/hi/world/middle_east/6455969.stm (accessed 12 Jun 2007).

Jones, S, *Building Cultural Literacy* (London: Demos, 2007), www.demos.co.uk/publications//buildingculturalliteracy (accessed 8 Nov 2008).

Jones, S, 'Change of culture', *Public Sector Review*, issue 9, Oct 2008.

Jones, S, 'The new cultural professionals' in Craig, J, *Production Values: Futures for professionalism* (London: Demos, 2006).

Kennedy, M, 'How Victorian restorers faked the clothes that seemed to show Hadrian's softer side', *Guardian*, 9 Jun 2008, www.guardian.co.uk/artanddesign/2008/jun/09/heritage.art (accessed 14 Aug 2008).

Kitto, S and Edge, D, 'The future of Indian arms and armour', *Icon News*, 13, Nov 2007.

Larsen, R, 'Conservation-restoration education in the light of the European Qualification Framework for Life Long Learning', *Journal for Conservation-Restoration Education* 1 (2008).

Lawson, M, 'Who cares what the reviewers say?', *Guardian*, 24 May 2006, www.guardian.co.uk/film/2006/may/24/culture.comment (accessed 18 Aug 2008).

Leadbeater, C, *We-Think: Mass innovation, not mass-production* (London: Profile, 2008).

Leadbeater, C, Bartlett, J and Gallagher, N, *Making it Personal* (London: Demos, 2008).

Lithgow, K, 'Developing conservation skills for the future in the National Trust', speaking at '20:20 Vision – the Conservation Workforce of the Future', 9 Jan 2008, Tate Modern, www.icon.org.uk/index.php?option=com_content&task=view&id=646&Itemid=103 (accessed 13 Aug 2008).

Lowenthal, D, 'Stewarding the past in a perplexing present' in Avrami, E, Mason, R and de la Torre, M, *Values and Heritage Conservation* (Los Angeles, CA: Getty Conservation Institute, 2000).

McMaster, B, *Supporting Excellence in the Arts: From measurement to judgement* (London: Department for Culture, Media and Sport, 2008).

Miliband, D, 'New diplomacy: challenges for foreign policy', speech to Chatham House, 19 Jul 2007.

Miller, P and Skidmore, P, *Disorganisation: Why future organisations must 'loosen up'* (London: Demos, 2004).

Mulgan, G, *Good and Bad Power: The ideals and betrayals of government* (London: Allen Lane, 2006).

Museums Association, *Pay in Museums* (London: Museums Association, 2008), www.museumsassociation.org/asset_arena/text/ry/policy_salarysurvey2004summary.pdf (accessed 19 May 2008).

National Museum Directors' Conference, *Values and Vision: The contribution of culture* (London: NMDC, 2006).

National Museum Directors' Conference, Museums, Libraries and Archives Council and Arts Council England, *Private Giving for the Public Good* (London: NMDC, MLA and ACE, 2008).

Neuberger, J, 'Volunteering in the public services: health and social care' (London: Cabinet Office, 2008), www.cabinetoffice.gov.uk/third_sector/news/news_releases/080310_volunteering.aspx (accessed 20 May 2008).

O'Leary, D, *The Politics of Public Behaviour* (London: Demos, 2008).

Osborne, G, 'Nudge, nudge, win, win', *Guardian*, 14 Jul 2008, www.guardian.co.uk/commentisfree/2008/jul/14/conservatives.economy?gusrc=rss&feed=politics (accessed 12 Aug 2008).

Parker, S, Spires, P, Mean, M and Farook, F, *State of Trust: How to build better relationships between councils and the public* (London: Demos, 2008).

Prime Minister's Strategy Unit, *Personal Responsibility and Changing Behaviour: The state of knowledge and its implications for policy* (London: Prime Minister's Strategy Unit, 2004).

Putnam, R, *Bowling Alone* (New York, Simon and Schuster, 2000).

Putnam, R, 'E pluribus unum: diversity and community in the twenty-first century', the 2006 Johan Skytte Prize Lecture, *Scandinavian Political Studies* 30, no 2 (2007).

Pye, E, 'The benefits of access through handling outweigh risks' in Saunders, D, Townsend, J and Woodcock, S, *Conservation and Access: Contributions to the London Congress*, 15–19 Sep (Dorchester: International Institute for Conservation of Historic and Artistic Works, 2008).

Pye, E and Sully, D, 'Evolving challenges, developing skills', *The Conservator* 30 (2007).

Sen, A, 'How does culture matter?' in Rao, V and Walton, M, *Culture and Public Action* (Stanford, CA: Stanford University Press, 2004).

Sennett, R, *The Craftsman* (London: Allen Lane, 2008).

Sennett, R, *The Fall of Public Man* (London: Penguin, 2002).

Shenton, H, 'Public engagement with conservation at the British Library' in Saunders, D, Townsend, J and Woodcock, S, *Conservation and Access: Contributions to the London Congress*, 15–19 Sep (Dorchester: International Institute for Conservation of Historic and Artistic Works, 2008).

Shirky, C, *Here Comes Everybody* (London: Allen Lane, 2008).

Stilgoe, J, Irwin, A and Jones, K, *The Received Wisdom: Opening up expert advice* (London: Demos, 2006).

Sully, D (ed), *Decolonising Conservation: Caring for Maori meeting houses outside New Zealand* (Walnut Creek, CA: Left Coast Press, 2007).

Tait, S, 'Textile conservation centre stitched up', *The Times*, 3 Dec 2007.

Taylor, C, 'Are you happy? Rob Dulstone, video-game restorer', *Guardian*, weekend supplement, 15 Mar 2008.

Thaler, R and Sunstein, C, *Nudge: Improving decisions about health, wealth, and happiness* (New Haven and London: Yale University Press, 2008).

Wilson, D, *The British Museum: Purpose and politics* (London: British Museum, 1989).

Demos – Licence to Publish

The work (as defined below) is provided under the terms of this licence ('licence'). The work is protected by copyright and/or other applicable law. Any use of the work other than as authorized under this licence is prohibited. By exercising any rights to the work provided here, you accept and agree to be bound by the terms of this licence. Demos grants you the rights contained here in consideration of your acceptance of such terms and conditions.

1   Definitions

A   **'Collective Work'** means a work, such as a periodical issue, anthology or encyclopedia, in which the Work in its entirety in unmodified form, along with a number of other contributions, constituting separate and independent works in themselves, are assembled into a collective whole. A work that constitutes a Collective Work will not be considered a Derivative Work (as defined below) for the purposes of this Licence.

B   **'Derivative Work'** means a work based upon the Work or upon the Work and other pre-existing works, such as a musical arrangement, dramatization, fictionalization, motion picture version, sound recording, art reproduction, abridgment, condensation, or any other form in which the Work may be recast, transformed, or adapted, except that a work that constitutes a Collective Work or a translation from English into another language will not be considered a Derivative Work for the purpose of this Licence.

C   **'Licensor'** means the individual or entity that offers the Work under the terms of this Licence.

D   **'Original Author'** means the individual or entity who created the Work.

E   **'Work'** means the copyrightable work of authorship offered under the terms of this Licence.

F   **'You'** means an individual or entity exercising rights under this Licence who has not previously violated the terms of this Licence with respect to the Work,or who has received express permission from Demos to exercise rights under this Licence despite a previous violation.

2   Fair Use Rights

Nothing in this licence is intended to reduce, limit, or restrict any rights arising from fair use, first sale or other limitations on the exclusive rights of the copyright owner under copyright law or other applicable laws.

3   Licence Grant

Subject to the terms and conditions of this Licence, Licensor hereby grants You a worldwide, royalty-free, non-exclusive,perpetual (for the duration of the applicable copyright) licence to exercise the rights in the Work as stated below:

A   to reproduce the Work, to incorporate the Work into one or more Collective Works, and to reproduce the Work as incorporated in the Collective Works;

B   to distribute copies or phonorecords of, display publicly,perform publicly, and perform publicly by means of a digital audio transmission the Work including as incorporated in Collective Works; The above rights may be exercised in all media and formats whether now known or hereafter devised.The above rights include the right to make such modifications as are technically necessary to exercise the rights in other media and formats. All rights not expressly granted by Licensor are hereby reserved.

4   Restrictions

The licence granted in Section 3 above is expressly made subject to and limited by the following restrictions:

A   You may distribute,publicly display, publicly perform, or publicly digitally perform the Work only under the terms of this Licence, and You must include a copy of, or the Uniform Resource Identifier for, this Licence with every copy or phonorecord of the Work You distribute, publicly display,publicly perform, or publicly digitally perform.You may not offer or impose any terms on the Work that alter or restrict the terms of this Licence or the recipients' exercise of the rights granted hereunder.You may not sublicence the Work.You must keep intact all notices that refer to this Licence and to the disclaimer of warranties.You may not distribute, publicly display, publicly perform, or publicly digitally perform the Work with any technological measures that control access or use of the Work in a manner inconsistent with the terms of this Licence Agreement.The above applies to the Work as incorporated in a Collective Work, but this does not require the Collective Work apart from the Work itself to be made subject to the terms of this Licence. If You create a Collective Work, upon notice from any Licencor You must, to the extent practicable, remove from the Collective Work any reference to such Licensor or the Original Author, as requested.

B   You may not exercise any of the rights granted to You in Section 3 above in any manner that is primarily intended for or directed toward commercial advantage or private monetary compensation.The exchange of the Work for other copyrighted works by means of digital filesharing or otherwise shall not be considered to be intended for or directed toward commercial advantage or private monetary compensation, provided there is no payment of any monetary compensation in connection with the exchange of copyrighted works.

c   If you distribute, publicly display, publicly perform, or publicly digitally perform the Work or any Collective Works,You must keep intact all copyright notices for the Work and give the Original Author credit reasonable to the medium or means You are utilizing by conveying the name (or pseudonym if applicable) of the Original Author if supplied; the title of the Work if supplied. Such credit may be implemented in any reasonable manner; provided, however, that in the case of a Collective Work, at a minimum such credit will appear where any other comparable authorship credit appears and in a manner at least as prominent as such other comparable authorship credit.

5   Representations, Warranties and Disclaimer

A   By offering the Work for public release under this Licence, Licensor represents and warrants that, to the best of Licensor's knowledge after reasonable inquiry:
  i   Licensor has secured all rights in the Work necessary to grant the licence rights hereunder and to permit the lawful exercise of the rights granted hereunder without You having any obligation to pay any royalties, compulsory licence fees, residuals or any other payments;
  ii The Work does not infringe the copyright, trademark, publicity rights, common law rights or any other right of any third party or constitute defamation, invasion of privacy or other tortious injury to any third party.

B   except as expressly stated in this licence or otherwise agreed in writing or required by applicable law,the work is licenced on an 'as is'basis,without warranties of any kind, either express or implied including,without limitation,any warranties regarding the contents or accuracy of the work.

6   Limitation on Liability

Except to the extent required by applicable law, and except for damages arising from liability to a third party resulting from breach of the warranties in section 5, in no event will licensor be liable to you on any legal theory for any special, incidental,consequential, punitive or exemplary damages arising out of this licence or the use of the work, even if licensor has been advised of the possibility of such damages.

7   Termination

A   This Licence and the rights granted hereunder will terminate automatically upon any breach by You of the terms of this Licence. Individuals or entities who have received Collective Works from You under this Licence,however, will not have their licences terminated provided such individuals or entities remain in full compliance with those licences. Sections 1, 2, 5, 6, 7, and 8 will survive any termination of this Licence.

B   Subject to the above terms and conditions, the licence granted here is perpetual (for the duration of the applicable copyright in the Work). Notwithstanding the above, Licensor reserves the right to release the Work under different licence terms or to stop distributing the Work at any time; provided, however that any such election will not serve to withdraw this Licence (or any other licence that has been, or is required to be, granted under the terms of this Licence), and this Licence will continue in full force and effect unless terminated as stated above.

8   Miscellaneous

A   Each time You distribute or publicly digitally perform the Work or a Collective Work, Demos offers to the recipient a licence to the Work on the same terms and conditions as the licence granted to You under this Licence.

B   If any provision of this Licence is invalid or unenforceable under applicable law, it shall not affect the validity or enforceability of the remainder of the terms of this Licence, and without further action by the parties to this agreement, such provision shall be reformed to the minimum extent necessary to make such provision valid and enforceable.

C   No term or provision of this Licence shall be deemed waived and no breach consented to unless such waiver or consent shall be in writing and signed by the party to be charged with such waiver or consent.

D   This Licence constitutes the entire agreement between the parties with respect to the Work licensed here.There are no understandings, agreements or representations with respect to the Work not specified here. Licensor shall not be bound by any additional provisions that may appear in any communication from You.This Licence may not be modified without the mutual written agreement of Demos and You.